A PURITA

NEW I

A Puritan Family Devotional

for family & individual meditations, containing:

Robert Murray M'Cheyne's

DAILY BREAD

Charles Haddon Spurgeon's

A PURITAN CATECHISM

the

1689 LONDON BAPTIST CONFESSION

and

SELECTED HYMNS & PSALMS

"Hear, O Israel: The LORD our God, the LORD is one! You shall love the LORD your God with all your heart, with all your soul, and with all your strength. And these words which I command you today shall be in your heart. You shall teach them diligently to your children, and shall talk of them when you sit in your house, when you walk by the way, when you lie down, and when you rise up. You shall bind them as a sign on your hand, and they shall be as frontlets between your eyes. You shall write them on the doorposts of your house and on your gates."

–Deuteronomy 6:4-9

Compiled & Edited by

JON J. CARDWELL

A Puritan Family Devotional
New King James Version

Published by Vayahiy Press

Printed by CreateSpace in the United States of America

CONTENTS

1.

CATECHISM INTRODUCTION & INSTRUCTION

C. H. Spurgeon's Introduction and Exhortation.

"I AM PERSUADED that the use of a good Catechism in all our families will be a great safeguard against the increasing errors of the times, and therefore I have compiled this little manual from the Westminster Assembly's and Baptist Catechisms, for the use of my own church and congregation. Those who use it in their families or classes must labour to explain the sense; but the words should be carefully learned by heart, for they will be understood better as years pass.

"May the Lord bless my dear friends and their families evermore, is the prayer of their loving Pastor."

—CHARLES H. SPURGEON
Pastor,
Metropolitan Tabernacle
LONDON

J. J. Cardwell's Introduction and Instruction.

INTRODUCTION.

A Puritan Catechism was published about October 14, 1855, when Charles Spurgeon was 21 years old. On October 14, Mr. Spurgeon preached "The Glorious Habitation" (Sermon No. 46) to thousands that gathered to hear him at New Park Street Chapel in Southwark. The text that morning was, *"Lord, Thou hast been our dwelling place in all generations"* (Psalm 90:1, KJV). When the penny publication for this sermon was published it contained an announcement of this catechism.

INSTRUCTION.

WITH THE CENTRALITY OF GOD'S WORD so dear to the Puritans, one might think that we would begin with the Scripture readings from R. M. McCheyne's *Daily Bread* first. If you are so inclined, and moved within your soul by the Holy Spirit, by all means do so. What we have found to be very effectual for our family, however, is reciting portions of the catechism following our opening prayer; and then, reading our Scripture portions from the *Daily Bread* afterward. The reason for this, we have found for our family at least, is through the united recitation of the catechism, we seem to be more of one accord in our devotional family worship unto the Lord: Father reciting the question, and all in unison, reciting the answer to that question. This would be somewhat akin to a responsive reading in worship. Therefore, the Holy Scriptures may be better received when read.

Although there may be many possibilities with regard to parsing the recitation of the catechism, I have only two suggestions. You may actually choose something different from what I suggest; and that's quite alright.

1. Having 82 questions and answers, the family can recite 3 questions and answers each day, enabling you to complete the Catechism once in 27 days and 12 times each year. For the remaining days of the month, the family can read the Scripture proofs for 3 to 4 answers each day with the head of the family asking simple questions to clarify understanding. In this way, the

Scripture proofs and doctrinal truths may be grasped more and more as each year passes.

2. The other method I might suggest would be to recite a page of the catechism each time you gather for devotions. For example, if you recite page 7 in the morning, recite the next page for devotions the following morning (that is, if you are using the Baptist Confession for reading during the evening devotions; otherwise, recite the next page during the evening devotions.

May our Lord bless you always in all ways as you grow in grace and faith.

JON J. CARDWELL.
Pastor,
Sovereign Grace Baptist Church
ANNISTON, ALABAMA

2.

A PURITAN CATECHISM

"Be diligent to present yourself approved to God, a worker who does not need to be ashamed, rightly dividing the word of truth."

—2 Timothy 2:15

Q1. What is the ultimate goal of man?
A. Man's ultimate goal is to glorify God,[1] and to enjoy Him forever.[2]

Q2. What instruction has God given to direct us how we may glorify Him?
A. The Word of God, which is contained in the Scriptures of the Old and New Testaments,[3] is the only instruction given to direct us how we may glorify God and enjoy Him.[4]

Q3. What do the Scriptures mainly teach?
A. The Scriptures mainly teach what man is to believe concerning God, and what duty God requires of man.[5]

Q4. What is God?
A. God is a Spirit,[6] infinite,[7] eternal,[8] and unchangeable,[9] in His being,[10] wisdom, power,[11] holiness,[12] justice, goodness, and truth.[13]

Q5. Are there more Gods than one?
A. There is only one,[14] the living and true God.[15]

Q6. How many persons are there in the Godhead?
A. There are three Persons in the Godhead, the Father, the Son, and the Holy Spirit, and these three are one God, the same in essence, equal in power and glory.[16]

Q7. What are the decrees of God?
A. The decrees of God are His eternal purpose according to the counsel of His own will, in which He has decided and ordained ahead of time whatever comes to pass, so that He alone is glorified.[17]

Q8. How does God accomplish His decrees?
A. God accomplishes His decrees in the works of creation[18] and providence.[19]

Q9. What is the work of creation?
A. The work of creation is God's making all things[20] from nothing, by the Word of His power,[21] in six normal consecutive days,[22] and

all very good.[23]

Q10. How did God create man?
A. God created man, male and female, after His own image,[24] in knowledge, righteousness, and holiness,[25] with dominion over the creatures.[26]

Q11. What are God's works of providence?
A. God's works of providence are His most holy,[27] wise,[28] and powerful[29] preserving and governing all His creatures, and all their actions.[30]

Q12. What special act of providence did God exercise toward man when He created him in his initial state?
A. When God had created man, He entered into a covenant of life with him, that upon condition of perfect obedience,[31] man was forbidden to eat from the tree of the knowledge of good and evil, upon pain of death.[32]

Q13. Did our first parents continue in the initial state that God had created them?
A. Being left to the freedom of their own will, our first parents fell from that initial state in which they were created, by sinning against God,[33] by eating the forbidden fruit.[34]

Q14. What is sin?
A. Sin is any lack of conformity to the law of God, or transgression against His law.[35]

Q15. Did all mankind fall in Adam's first transgression?
A. The covenant being made with Adam, not only for himself but also for his posterity, all mankind descending from him by ordinary generation, sinned in him, and fell with him in his first transgression.[36]

Q16. What state of circumstances did the fall bring to mankind?
A. The fall brought mankind into a state of sin and misery.[37]

Q17. What does the sinfulness of man's fallen state consist of?
A. The sinfulness of man's fallen state consists of the guilt of Adam's first sin,[38] the lack of original righteousness,[39] and the corruption of his whole nature, which is commonly called original sin;[40] together with all actual transgressions which proceed from it.[41]

Q18. What is the misery of man's fallen state?
A. All mankind, by their fall, lost communion with God,[42] are under His wrath and curse,[43] therefore, all mankind is made answerable to all the miseries in this life, to death itself, and to the pains of hell forever.[44]

Q19. Did God leave all mankind to perish in the state of sin and misery?
A. God, having out of His good pleasure from all eternity, elected some to everlasting life,[45] entered into a covenant of grace to deliver them out of the state of sin and misery, and to bring them into a state of salvation by a Redeemer.[46]

Q20. Who is the Redeemer of God's elect?
A. The only Redeemer of God's elect is the Lord Jesus Christ,[47] who being the eternal Son of God became man,[48] and so was and continues to be God and man, in two distinct natures and one Person, forever.[49]

Q21. How did Christ, being the Son of God, become man?
A. Christ, the Son of God, became man by taking to Himself a true body,[50] and a reasonable soul,[51] being conceived by the power of the Holy Ghost in the Virgin Mary, and born of her,[52] yet without sin.[53]

Q22. What offices does Christ execute as our Redeemer?
A. Christ, as our Redeemer, executes the offices of a prophet,[54] of a priest,[55] and of a king,[56] both in His state of humiliation and exaltation.

Q23. How does Christ execute the office of a prophet?
A. Christ executes the office of a prophet, in revealing to us,[57] by His Word[58] and Spirit,[59] the will of God for our salvation.

Q24. How does Christ execute the office of a priest?
A. Christ executes the office of a priest, in His once offering up Himself a sacrifice to satisfy divine justice,[60] reconciling us to God,[61] and in making continual intercession for us.[62]

Q25. How does Christ execute the office of a king?
A. Christ executes the office of a king by bringing us into submission to Himself,[63] in ruling and defending us,[64] and in restraining and conquering all His and our enemies.

Q26. Of what did Christ's humiliation consist?
A. Christ's humiliation consisted in His being born, and that in a low condition,[65] made under the law,[66] undergoing the miseries of this life,[67] the wrath of God,[68] and the cursed death of the cross;[69] in being buried, and continuing under the power of death for a time.[70]

Q27. Of what did Christ's exaltation consist?
A. Christ's exaltation consists of His rising again from the dead on the third day,[71] in ascending up into heaven and sitting at the right hand of God the Father,[72] and in coming to judge the world at the last day.[73]

Q28. How are we made partakers of the redemption purchased by Christ?
A. We are made partakers of the redemption purchased by Christ, by the persuasive and effective application of it to us[74] by His Holy Spirit.[75]

Q29. How does the Spirit apply to us the redemption purchased by Christ?
A. The Spirit applies to us the redemption purchased by Christ, by working faith in us,[76] and by it, uniting us to Christ in our effectual calling.[77]

Q30. What is effectual calling?
A. Effectual calling is the work of God's Spirit,[78] in which He convinces us of our sin and misery,[79] enlightens our minds in the knowledge of Christ,[80] renews our wills,[81] and persuades and enables us to embrace Jesus Christ freely offered to us in the gospel.[82]

Q31. What benefits do they who are effectually called partake of in this life?
A. They that are effectually called in this life partake of justification,[83] adoption,[84] and sanctification, as well as the various benefits that either accompany or flow from them in this life.[85]

Q32. What is justification?
A. Justification is an act of God's free grace, in which He pardons all our sins,[86] and accepts us as righteous in His sight,[87] only because of the righteousness of Christ imputed to us,[88] and that, received by faith alone.[89]

Q33. What is adoption?
A. Adoption is an act of God's free grace,[90] in which we are received into the number of those effectually called, and have a right to all the privileges of the sons of God.[91]

Q34. What is sanctification?
A. Sanctification is the work of God's free grace,[92] in which we are renewed in the whole man after the image of God,[93] and are enabled more and more to die to sin, and live to righteousness.[94]

Q35. What are the benefits that either accompany or flow from justification, adoption, and sanctification in this life?
A. The benefits that accompany or flow from justification, adoption, and sanctification[95] in this life are assurance of God's love, peace of conscience, joy in the Holy Spirit,[96] increase of grace, and perseverance in it to the end.[97]

Q36. What benefits do believers receive from Christ at death?

A. The souls of believers are made perfect in holiness at their death,[98] and immediately pass into glory;[99] and being still united to Christ, their bodies,[100] rest in their graves,[101] until the resurrection.[102]

Q37. What benefits do believers receive from Christ at the resurrection?
A. At the resurrection, believers, being raised up in glory,[103] shall be openly acknowledged and acquitted in the day of judgment,[104] and made perfectly blessed both in soul and body, fully enjoying God[105] for all eternity.[106]

Q38. What shall be done to the wicked at their death?
A. The souls of the wicked shall be cast into the torments of hell at their death;[107] and their bodies will lie in their graves until the resurrection, and judgment of the great day.[108]

Q39. What shall be done to the wicked at the day of judgment?
A. At the day of judgment, the bodies of the wicked will be raised out of their graves, and they shall be sentenced to unspeakable torments with the devil and his angels for ever.[109]

Q40. What did God reveal to man for the rule of his obedience?
A. The rule which God first revealed to man for his obedience is the moral law, which is summarized in the Ten Commandments.[110]

Q41. What is the sum of the Ten Commandments?
A. The sum of the Ten Commandments is to love the Lord our God with all our heart, with all our soul, with all our strength, and with all our mind; and our neighbor as ourselves.[111]

Q42. What is the first commandment?
A. The first commandment is, *"You shall have no other gods before Me."*[112]

Q43. What is required in the first commandment?
A. The first commandment requires us to know[113] and

acknowledge God to be the only true God, that He is our God,[114] and to worship and glorify Him accordingly.[115]

Q44. What is the second commandment?

A. The second commandment is, *"You shall not make for yourself a carved image, or any likeness of anything that is in heaven above, or that is in the earth beneath, or that is in the water under the earth; you shall not bow down to them nor serve them. For I, the LORD your God, am a jealous God, visiting the iniquity of the fathers on the children to the third and fourth generations of those who hate Me, but showing mercy to thousands, to those who love Me and keep My commandments."*[116]

Q45. What is required in the second commandment?

A. The second commandment requires that we receive and observe,[117] and keep pure and entire all such religious worship and ordinances as God has appointed in His Word.[118]

Q46. What is forbidden in the second commandment?

A. The second commandment forbids the worship of God by use of images,[119] or any other way not appointed in His Word.[120]

Q47. What is the third commandment?

A. The third commandment is, *"You shall not take the name of the LORD your God in vain, for the LORD will not hold him guiltless who takes His name in vain."*[121]

Q48. What is required in the third commandment?

A. The third commandment requires the holy and reverent use of God's names,[122] titles, attributes,[123] ordinances,[124] Word,[125] and works.[126]

Q49. What is the fourth commandment?

A. The fourth commandment is, *"Remember the Sabbath day, to keep it holy. Six days you shall labor and do all your work, but the seventh day is the Sabbath of the LORD your God. In it you shall do no work: you, nor your son, nor your daughter, nor your male servant, nor your female servant, nor your cattle, nor your stranger who is within your gates. For in six days the LORD made the heavens and the earth, the sea, and all that is in them, and rested the seventh day. Therefore the LORD blessed the Sabbath day and hallowed it."*[127]

Q50. What is required in the fourth commandment?
A. The fourth commandment requires that such set times as God has appointed in His Word are kept holy unto Him, expressly one whole day in seven as a holy Sabbath to Himself.[128]

Q51. How is the Sabbath to be sanctified?
A. The Sabbath is to be sanctified by a holy resting all that day, even from such worldly employments and recreations as are lawful on other days;[129] and spending the whole time in the public and private exercises of God's worship,[130] except so much as is taken up in the works of necessity and mercy.[131]

Q52. What is the fifth commandment?
A. The fifth commandment is, *"Honor your father and your mother, that your days may be long upon the land which the LORD your God is giving you."*[132]

Q53. What is required in the fifth commandment?
A. The fifth commandment requires preserving the honor, and performing the duties belonging to every person in their various positions and relationships as superiors,[133] inferiors,[134] or equals.[135]

Q54. What is the reason attached to the fifth commandment?
A. The reason attached to the fifth commandment is a promise of long life and prosperity— as far as it shall serve for God's glory, and for his or her own good— to all such as keep this commandment.[136]

Q55. What is the sixth commandment?
A. The sixth commandment is, *"You shall not murder."*[137]

Q56. What is forbidden in the sixth commandment?
A. The sixth commandment forbids the taking away of our own

life,[138] the life of our neighbor unjustly,[139] or whatever has a tendency toward it.[140]

Q57. What is the seventh commandment?
A. The seventh commandment is, *"You shall not commit adultery."*[141]

Q58. What is forbidden in the seventh commandment?
A. The seventh commandment forbids all impure thoughts,[142] words,[143] and actions.[144]

Q59. What is the eighth commandment?
A. The eighth commandment is, *"You shall not steal."*[145]

Q60. What is forbidden in the eighth commandment?
A. The eighth commandment forbids whatever does or may unjustly hinder our own[146] or our neighbor's wealth, or outward circumstances.[147]

Q61. What is the ninth commandment?
A. The ninth commandment is, *"You shall not bear false witness against your neighbor."*[148]

Q62. What is required in the ninth commandment?
A. The ninth commandment requires maintaining and promoting the truth between man and man,[149] for the sake of our own good name,[150] and that of our neighbor's,[151] especially in witness-bearing.[152]

Q63. What is the tenth commandment?
A. The tenth commandment is, *"You shall not covet your neighbor's house; you shall not covet your neighbor's wife, nor his male servant, nor his female servant, nor his ox, nor his donkey, nor anything that is your neighbor's."*[153]

Q64. What is forbidden in the tenth commandment?
A. The tenth commandment forbids all discontentment with our own estate,[154] envying or grieving at the good of our neighbor,[155] and all inordinate motions and affections to anything that belongs

to him.[156]

Q65. Is any man able to perfectly keep the commandments of God?
A. No mere man, since the fall, is able to perfectly keep the commandments of God in his life,[157] but daily breaks them in thought,[158] word,[159] and deed.[160]

Q66. Are all transgressions of the law equally heinous?
A. Some sins in themselves, and by reason of various aggravations, are more heinous in the sight of God than others.[161]

Q67. What does every sin deserve?
A. Every sin deserves God's wrath and curse, both in this life, and that which is to come.[162]

Q68. How may we escape His wrath and curse due to us for sin?
A. To escape the wrath and curse of God due to us for sin, we must believe in the Lord Jesus Christ,[163] trusting alone to His blood and righteousness. This faith is accompanied by repentance for the past[164] and leads to holiness in the future.

Q69. What is faith in Jesus Christ?
A. Faith in Jesus Christ is a saving grace,[165] in which we receive[166] and rest upon Him alone for salvation,[167] as He is set forth in the gospel.[168]

Q70. What is repentance unto life?
A. Repentance unto life is a saving grace,[169] in which a sinner, out of a true sense of his sin,[170] and apprehension of the mercy of God in Christ,[171] does with grief and hatred of his sin, turn from it unto God,[172] with full purpose to strive after new obedience.[173]

Q71. What are the outward means by which the Holy Spirit communicates to us the benefits of redemption?
A. The outward and ordinary means by which the Holy Spirit communicates to us the benefits of Christ's redemption are the Word, by which souls are begotten to spiritual life; Baptism, the

Lord's Supper, Prayer, and Meditation, by all which believers are further edified in their most holy faith.[174]

Q72. How is the Word made powerful and effective to salvation?
A. The Spirit of God makes the reading, but especially the preaching of the Word, an effectual means of convicting and converting sinners,[175] and of building them up in holiness and comfort[176] through faith to salvation.[177]

Q73. How is the Word to be read and heard that it may become powerful and effective to salvation?
A. That the Word may become powerful and effective to salvation, we must give attention to it with diligence,[178] preparation,[179] and prayer,[180] receive it with faith[181] and love,[182] lay it up into our hearts,[183] and practice it in our lives.[184]

Q74. How do Baptism and the Lord's Supper become spiritually helpful?
A. Baptism and the Lord's Supper become spiritually helpful, not from any virtue in them, or in him who does administer them,[185] but only by the blessing of Christ,[186] and the working of the Spirit in those who receive them by faith.[187]

Q75. What is Baptism?
A. Baptism is an ordinance of the New Testament instituted by Jesus Christ,[188] to be to the person baptized a sign of his fellowship with Him in His death, burial, and resurrection,[189] of his being engrafted into Him,[190] of forgiveness of sins,[191] and of his giving up himself to God through Jesus Christ, to live and walk in newness of life.[192]

Q76. To whom is Baptism to be administered?
A. Baptism is to be administered to all those who actually profess repentance towards God,[193] and faith in our Lord Jesus Christ, and to no one else.

Q77. Are the infants of those professing faith to be baptized?

A. The infants of those professing believers are not to be baptized because there is neither command nor example in the Holy Scriptures for their baptism.[194]

Q78. How is Baptism rightly administered?
A. Baptism is rightly administered by immersion, or dipping the whole body of the person in water,[195] in the name of the Father, and of the Son, and of the Holy Spirit, according to Christ's institution, and the practice of the apostles,[196] and not by sprinkling or pouring of water, or dipping some part of the body, after the tradition of men.[197]

Q79. What is the duty of those who have been rightly baptized?
A. It is the duty of those who are rightly baptized to give themselves up to some particular and orderly Church of Jesus Christ[198] that they may walk in all the commandments and ordinances of the Lord blameless.[199]

Q80. What is the Lord's Supper?
A. The Lord's Supper is an ordinance of the New Testament, instituted by Jesus Christ; in which, by giving and receiving bread and wine according to His appointment, His death is proclaimed;[200] and the worthy receivers are made partakers of His body and blood, not after a corporeal and carnal manner, but by faith, with all His benefits, to their spiritual nourishment, and growth in grace.[201]

Q81. What is required for the worthy receiving of the Lord's Supper?
A. It is required of them who would worthily partake of the Lord's Supper, that they examine themselves of their knowledge to discern the Lord's body,[202] of their faith to feed upon Him,[203] of their repentance,[204] love,[205] and new obedience;[206] for fear that coming unworthily, they eat and drink judgment to themselves.[207]

Q82. What is meant by the words, *"till He comes,"* which are used by the apostle Paul in reference to the Lord's Supper?

A. They plainly teach us that our Lord Jesus Christ will come a second time, which is the joy and hope of all believers.[208]

---

[1] 1 Corinthians 10:31
[2] Psalm 73:25, 26
[3] Ephesians 2:20; 2 Timothy 3:16
[4] 1 John 1:3, 4
[5] Ecclesiastes 12:13; 2 Timothy 1:13
[6] John 4:24
[7] Job 11:7
[8] Psalm 90:2; 1 Timothy 1:17
[9] James 1:17
[10] Exodus 3:14
[11] Psalm 147:5
[12] Revelation 4:8
[13] Exodus 34:6, 7
[14] Deuteronomy 6:4
[15] Jeremiah 10:10
[16] Matthew 28:19; 1 John 5:7 (Although it is not included in newer translations such as the NIV, NLT, and etc., the KJV and the NKJV contain the following words that have been translated from the "majority texts" of the Greek manuscripts: *"For there are three that bear record in heaven, the Father, the Word, and the Holy Ghost: and these three are one."* There are certainly other passages that imply the triune Godhead in Scripture, i.e., the resurrection of Christ was accomplished by the Father (Ephesians 1:17-20), the Son (John 2:19), and the Holy Spirit (Romans 8:11). This doctrine is also referred to as "The Trinity.").
[17] Ephesians 1:11, 12
[18] Revelation 4:11
[19] Daniel 4:35
[20] Genesis 1:1
[21] Psalm 33:6, 9; Hebrews 11:3
[22] Exodus 20:11
[23] Genesis 1:31
[24] Genesis 1:27
[25] Ephesians 4:24; Colossians 3:10
[26] Genesis 1:28
[27] Psalm 145:17
[28] Isaiah 28:29
[29] Hebrews 1:3
[30] Psalm 103:19; Matthew 10:29
[31] Galatians 3:12
[32] Genesis 2:17
[33] Ecclesiastes 7:29
[34] Genesis 3:6-8
[35] 1 John 3:4

[36] Romans 5:12; 1 Corinthians 15:22
[37] Romans 5:18
[38] Romans 5:19
[39] Romans 3:10
[40] Psalm 51:5; Ephesians 2:1
[41] Matthew 15:19
[42] Genesis 3:8, 24
[43] Ephesians 2:3; Galatians 3:10
[44] Romans 6:23; Matthew 25:41
[45] 2 Thessalonians 2:13
[46] Romans 5:21
[47] 1 Timothy 2:5
[48] John 1:14
[49] 1 Timothy 3:16; Colossians 2:9
[50] Hebrews 2:14
[51] Matthew 26:38; Hebrews 4:15
[52] Luke 1:31, 35
[53] Hebrews 7:26
[54] Acts 3:22
[55] Hebrews 5:6
[56] Psalm 2:6
[57] John 1:18
[58] John 20:31
[59] John 14:26
[60] Hebrews 9:28
[61] Hebrews 2:17
[62] Hebrews 7:25
[63] Psalm 110:3
[64] Matthew 2:6; 1 Corinthians 15:25
[65] Luke 2:7
[66] Galatians 4:4
[67] Isaiah 53:3
[68] Matthew 27:46
[69] Philippians 2:8
[70] Matthew 12:40
[71] 1 Corinthians 15:4
[72] Mark 16:19
[73] Matthew 16:27; Acts 17:31
[74] John 1:12
[75] Titus 3:6, 6
[76] Ephesians 2:8
[77] Ephesians 3:17
[78] 2 Timothy 1:19
[79] Acts 2:37
[80] Acts 26:18
[81] Ezekiel 36:26, 27
[82] John 6:44, 45

[83] Romans 8:30
[84] Ephesians 1:5
[85] 1 Corinthians 1:30
[86] Romans 3:24; Ephesians 1:7
[87] 2 Corinthians 5:21
[88] Romans 5:19
[89] Galatians 2:16; Philippians 3:9
[90] 1 John 3:1
[91] John 1:12; Romans 8:17
[92] 2 Thessalonians 2:13
[93] Ephesians 4:24
[94] Romans 6:11
[95] Romans 5:1-2, 5
[96] Romans 14:17
[97] Philippians 4:18; 1 Peter 1:5; 1 John 5:13
[98] Hebrews 12:23
[99] Luke 23:43; 2 Corinthians 5:8; Philippians 1:23
[100] 1 Thessalonians 4:14
[101] Isaiah 57:2
[102] Job 19:26
[103] 1 Corinthians 15:43
[104] Matthew 10:32
[105] 1 John 3:2
[106] 1 Thessalonians 4:17
[107] Luke 16:22-24
[108] Psalm 49:14
[109] Daniel 12:2; John 5:28, 29; 2 Thessalonians 1:9; Matthew 25:41
[110] Deuteronomy 10:4; Matthew 19:17
[111] Matthew 22:37-40
[112] Exodus 20:3
[113] 1 Chronicles 28:9
[114] Deuteronomy 26:17
[115] Matthew 4:10
[116] Exodus 20:4-6
[117] Deuteronomy 32:46; Matthew 28:20
[118] Deuteronomy 12:32
[119] Deuteronomy 4:15, 16
[120] Colossians 2:18
[121] Exodus 20:7
[122] Psalm 29:2
[123] Revelation 15:3, 4
[124] Ecclesiastes 5:1
[125] Psalm 138:2
[126] Job 36:24; Deuteronomy 28:58, 59
[127] Exodus 20:8-11
[128] Leviticus 19:30; Deuteronomy 5:12
[129] Leviticus 23:3

[130] Psalm 92:1, 2; Isaiah 58:13, 14
[131] Matthew 12:11, 12
[132] Exodus 20:12
[133] Romans 13:1; Ephesians 5:21, 22; Ephesians 6:1, 5
[134] Ephesians 6:9
[135] Romans 12:10
[136] Ephesians 6:2, 3
[137] Exodus 20:13
[138] Acts 16:28
[139] Genesis 9:6
[140] Proverbs 24:11, 12
[141] Exodus 20:14
[142] Matthew 5:28; Colossians 4:6
[143] Ephesians 5:4; 2 Timothy 2:22
[144] Ephesians 5:3
[145] Exodus 20:15
[146] 1 Timothy 5:8; Proverbs 28:19; Proverbs 21:6
[147] Ephesians 4:28
[148] Exodus 20:16
[149] Zechariah 8:16
[150] 1 Peter 3:16; Acts 25:10
[151] 3 John 12
[152] Proverbs 14:5, 25
[153] Exodus 20:17
[154] 1 Corinthians 10:10
[155] Galatians 5:26
[156] Colossians 3:5
[157] Ecclesiastes 7:20
[158] Genesis 8:21
[159] James 3:8
[160] James 3:2
[161] John 19:11; 1 John 5:15
[162] Ephesians 5:6; Psalm 11:6
[163] John 3:16
[164] Acts 20:21
[165] Hebrews 10:39
[166] John 1:12
[167] Philippians 3:9
[168] Isaiah 33:22
[169] Acts 11:18
[170] Acts 2:37
[171] Joel 2:13
[172] Jeremiah 31:18, 19
[173] Psalm 119:59
[174] Acts 2:41, 42; James 1:18
[175] Psalm 19:7
[176] 1 Thessalonians 1:6

[177] Romans 1:16
[178] Proverbs 8:34
[179] 1 Peter 2:1, 2
[180] Psalm 119:18
[181] Hebrews 4:2
[182] 2 Thessalonians 2:10
[183] Psalm 119:11
[184] Hebrews 4:2; James 1:25
[185] 1 Corinthians 3:7; 1 Peter 3:21
[186] 1 Corinthians 3:6
[187] 1 Corinthians 12:13
[188] Matthew 28:19
[189] Romans 6:3; Colossians 2:12
[190] Galatians 3:27
[191] Mark 1:4; Acts 22:16
[192] Acts 2:38-42; Acts 22:16; Romans 6:4, 5; Galatians 3:26, 27; 1 Peter 3:21
[193] Acts 2:38; Matthew 3:6; Mark 16:16; Acts 8:12, 36, 37; Acts 10:47, 48
[194] Exodus 23:13; Proverbs 30:6
[195] Matthew 3:16; John 3:23
[196] Matthew 28:19, 20
[197] John 4:1, 2; Acts 8:38, 39
[198] Acts 2:47; 9:26; 1 Peter 2:5
[199] Luke 1:6
[200] 1 Corinthians 11:23-26
[201] 1 Corinthians 10:16
[202] 1 Corinthians 11:28, 29
[203] 2 Corinthians 13:5
[204] 1 Corinthians 11:31
[205] 1 Corinthians 11:18-20
[206] 1 Corinthians 5:8
[207] 1 Corinthians 11:27-29
[208] Acts 1:11; 1 Corinthians 11:26; 1 Thessalonians 4:16

3.

DAILY BREAD
INTRODUCTION & INSTRUCTION

J. J. Cardwell's Introduction.

"DAILY BREAD" WAS WRITTEN by Robert Murray M'Cheyne for the congregation at St. Peter's Church in Dundee, Scotland, and was presented to them on December 30, 1842 for use at the beginning of the calendar year. Our source for his message and calendar comes from *Memoir and Remains of the Rev. Robert Murray M'Cheyne, Minister of St. Peter's Church in Dundee* by Andrew Bonar.

R. M. McCheyne's Instructions.

BEING A CALENDAR FOR READING THROUGH THE WORD OF GOD IN A YEAR.

"Your word is very pure; therefore Your servant loves it."

MY DEAR FLOCK,— The approach of another year stirs up within me new desires for your salvation, and for the growth of those of you who are saved. *"For God is my witness, how I long for you all with the affection of Jesus Christ."* What the coming year is to bring forth, who can tell? There is plainly a weight lying on the spirits of all good men, and a looking for some strange work of judgment coming upon this land. There is need now to ask that solemn question: *"If in the land of peace, in which you trusted, they wearied you, then how will you do in the floodplain of Jordan?"*

Those believers will stand firmest who have no dependence upon self or upon creatures, but upon Jehovah our Righteousness. We must be driven more to our Bibles, and to the mercy seat, if we are to stand in the evil day. Then we shall be able to say, like David, *"The proud have me in great derision, yet I do not turn aside from Your law." "Princes persecute me without a cause, but my heart stands in awe of Your word."*

It has long been in my mind to prepare a scheme of Scripture reading, in which as many as were made willing by God might agree, so that the whole Bible might be read once by you in the year, and all might be feeding in the same portion of the green pasture at the same time.

I am quite aware that such a plan is accompanied with many...

DANGERS.

(1.) *Formality.* —We are such weak creatures that any regularly returning duty is apt to degenerate into a lifeless form. The tendency of reading the Word by a fixed rule may, in same minds, be to create this skeleton religion. This is to be the peculiar sin of the last days: *"having the form of godliness but denying its power."* Guard against this. Let the calendar perish rather than this rust eat up your souls.

(2.) *Self-righteousness.* —Some, when they have devoted their set time to reading the Word, and accomplished their prescribed portion, may be tempted to look at themselves with self-complacency. Many, I am persuaded, are living without any divine work on their soul— unpardoned and unsanctified, and ready to perish— who spend their appointed times in secret and family devotion. This is going to hell with a lie in the right hand.

(3.) *Careless reading.* —Few *tremble* at the Word of God. Few, in reading it, hear the voice of Jehovah, which is full of majesty. Some, by having so large a portion, may be tempted to weary of it, as Israel did of the daily manna, saying, *"Our soul loathes this worthless bread!"* and to read it in a slight and careless manner. This would be fearfully provoking to God. Take heed lest that word be true of you: *"You also say, 'Oh, what a weariness!' and you sneer at it," says the LORD of hosts."*

(4.) *A yoke too heavy to bear.* —Some may engage in reading with alacrity for a time, and afterwards feel it a burden, grievous to be borne. They may find conscience dragging them through the appointed task without any relish of the heavenly food. If this be the case with any, throw aside the fetter, and feed at liberty in the sweet garden of God. My desire is not to cast a snare upon you, but to be a helper of your joy.

If there be so many dangers, why propose such a scheme at all? To this I answer, that the best things are accompanied with danger, as the fairest flowers are often gathered in the clefts of some dangerous precipice. Let us weigh...

THE ADVANTAGES.

(1.) *The whole Bible will be read through in an orderly manner in the course of a year.* —The Old Testament once, the New Testament and Psalms twice. I fear many of you never read the whole Bible; and yet it is all equally divine: *"All Scripture is given by inspiration of God, and is profitable for doctrine, for reproof, for correction, for instruction in righteousness, that the man of God may be complete."* If we pass over some parts of Scripture, we shall be incomplete Christians.

(2.) *Time will not be wasted in choosing what portions to read.* —Often believers are at a loss to determine towards which part of the mountains of spices they should bend their steps. Here the question will be solved at once in a very simple manner.

(3.) *Parents will have a regular subject upon which to examine their children and servants.* —It is much to be desired that family worship were made more instructive than it generally is. The mere reading of the chapter is often too like water spilt on the ground. Let it be read by every member of the family beforehand, and then the meaning and application drawn out by simple question and answer. The calendar will be helpful in this. Friends, also, when they meet, will have a subject for profitable conversation in the portions read that day. The meaning of difficult passages may be inquired from the more judicious and ripe Christians, and the fragrance of simpler Scriptures spread abroad.

(4.) *The pastor will know in what part of the pasture the flock are feeding.* —He will thus be enabled to speak more suitably to them on the Sabbath; and both pastor and elders will be able to drop a word of light and comfort in visiting from house to house, which will be more readily responded to.

(5.) *The sweet bond of Christian love and unity will be strengthened.* —We shall be often led to think of those dear brothers and sisters in the Lord, here and elsewhere, who agree to join with us in reading these portions. We shall oftener be led to agree on earth, touching something we shall ask of God. We shall pray over the same promises, mourn over the same confessions, praise God in the same songs, and be nourished by the same words of eternal life.

CALENDAR DIRECTIONS.

1. The center column contains the day of the month. The two first columns contain the chapter to be read in the family. The two last columns contain the portions to be read in secret.
2. The head of the family should previously read over the chapter for family worship, and mark two or three of the most prominent verses, upon which he may dwell, asking a few simple questions.
3. Frequently the chapter named in the calendar for family reading might be read more suitably in secret; in which case the head of the family should intimate that it be read in private, and the chapter for secret reading may be used in the family.
4. The metrical version of the Psalms should be read or sung through at least once in the year. It is truly an admirable translation from the Hebrew, and is frequently more correct than the prose version. If three verses be sung at each diet of family worship, the whole Psalms will be sung though in the year.
5. Let the conversation at family meals often turn upon the chapter read and the psalm sung. Thus every meal will be a

sacrament, being sanctified by the Word and prayer.

6. Let our secret reading prevent the dawning of the day. Let God's voice be the first we hear in the morning. Mark two or three of the richest verses, and pray over every line and word of them. Let the marks be neatly done, never so as to abuse a copy of the Bible.

7. In meeting believers on the street or elsewhere, when an easy opportunity offers, recur to the chapters read that morning. This will be a blessed exchange for those *idle words* which waste the soul and grieve the Holy Spirit of God. In writing letters to those at a distance, make use of the provision that day gathered.

8. Above all, use the Word as a lamp to your feet and a light to your path— your guide in perplexity, your armour in temptation, your food in times of faintness. Hear the constant cry of the great Intercessor,

"SANCTIFY THEM BY YOUR TRUTH.
YOUR WORD IS TRUTH."

Rev. R.M. M'Cheyne
ST. PETER'S, DUNDEE, *30th Dec.* 1842

JANUARY

THIS IS MY BELOVED SON, IN WHOM I AM WELL PLEASED.
HEAR HIM!

FAMILY			SECRET	
Genesis 1	Matthew 1	**1**	Ezra 1	Acts 1
Genesis 2	Matthew 2	**2**	Ezra 2	Acts 2
Genesis 3	Matthew 3	**3**	Ezra 3	Acts 3
Genesis 4	Matthew 4	**4**	Ezra 4	Acts 4
Genesis 5	Matthew 5	**5**	Ezra 5	Acts 5
Genesis 6	Matthew 6	**6**	Ezra 6	Acts 6
Genesis 7	Matthew 7	**7**	Ezra 7	Acts 7
Genesis 8	Matthew 8	**8**	Ezra 8	Acts 8
Genesis 9-10	Matthew 9	**9**	Ezra 9	Acts 9
Genesis 11	Matthew 10	**10**	Ezra 10	Acts 10
Genesis 12	Matthew 11	**11**	Nehemiah 1	Acts 11
Genesis 13	Matthew 12	**12**	Nehemiah 2	Acts 12
Genesis 14	Matthew 13	**13**	Nehemiah 3	Acts 13
Genesis 15	Matthew 14	**14**	Nehemiah 4	Acts 14
Genesis 16	Matthew 15	**15**	Nehemiah 5	Acts 15
Genesis 17	Matthew 16	**16**	Nehemiah 6	Acts 16
Genesis 18	Matthew 17	**17**	Nehemiah 7	Acts 17
Genesis 19	Matthew 18	**18**	Nehemiah 8	Acts 18
Genesis 20	Matthew 19	**19**	Nehemiah 9	Acts 19
Genesis 21	Matthew 20	**20**	Nehemiah 10	Acts 20
Genesis 22	Matthew 21	**21**	Nehemiah 11	Acts 21
Genesis 23	Matthew 22	**22**	Nehemiah 12	Acts 22
Genesis 24	Matthew 23	**23**	Nehemiah 13	Acts 23
Genesis 25	Matthew 24	**24**	Esther 1	Acts 24
Genesis 26	Matthew 25	**25**	Esther 2	Acts 25
Genesis 27	Matthew 26	**26**	Esther 3	Acts 26
Genesis 28	Matthew 27	**27**	Esther 4	Acts 27
Genesis 29	Matthew 28	**28**	Esther 5	Acts 28
Genesis 30	Mark 1	**29**	Esther 6	Romans 1
Genesis 31	Mark 2	**30**	Esther 7	Romans 2
Genesis 32	Mark 3	**31**	Esther 8	Romans 3

FEBRUARY

I HAVE TREASURED THE WORDS OF HIS MOUTH MORE THAN MY NECESSARY FOOD.

FAMILY			SECRET	
Genesis 33	Mark 4	**1**	Esther 9-10	Romans 4
Genesis 34	Mark 5	**2**	Job 1	Romans 5
Genesis 35-36	Mark 6	**3**	Job 2	Romans 6
Genesis 37	Mark 7	**4**	Job 3	Romans 7
Genesis 38	Mark 8	**5**	Job 4	Romans 8
Genesis 39	Mark 9	**6**	Job 5	Romans 9
Genesis 40	Mark 10	**7**	Job 6	Romans 10
Genesis 41	Mark 11	**8**	Job 7	Romans 11
Genesis 42	Mark 12	**9**	Job 8	Romans 12
Genesis 43	Mark 13	**10**	Job 9	Romans 13
Genesis 44	Mark 14	**11**	Job 10	Romans 14
Genesis 45	Mark 15	**12**	Job 11	Romans 15
Genesis 46	Mark 16	**13**	Job 12	Romans 16
Genesis 47	Luke 1:1-38	**14**	Job 13	1 Cor. 1
Genesis 48	Luke 1:39-80	**15**	Job 14	1 Cor. 2
Genesis 49	Luke 2	**16**	Job 15	1 Cor. 3
Genesis 50	Luke 3	**17**	Job 16-17	1 Cor. 4
Exodus 1	Luke 4	**18**	Job 18	1 Cor. 5
Exodus 2	Luke 5	**19**	Job 19	1 Cor. 6
Exodus 3	Luke 6	**20**	Job 20	1 Cor. 7
Exodus 4	Luke 7	**21**	Job 21	1 Cor. 8
Exodus 5	Luke 8	**22**	Job 22	1 Cor. 9
Exodus 6	Luke 9	**23**	Job 23	1 Cor. 10
Exodus 7	Luke 10	**24**	Job 24	1 Cor. 11
Exodus 8	Luke 11	**25**	Job 25-26	1 Cor. 12
Exodus 9	Luke 12	**26**	Job 27	1 Cor. 13
Exodus 10	Luke 13	**27**	Job 28	1 Cor. 14
Ex. 11-12:21	Luke 14	**28**	Job 29	1 Cor. 15

Abbreviations: Ex. – Exodus; 1 Cor. – 1 Corinthians

LEAP YEAR – FEBRUARY/MARCH

FAMILY			SECRET	
Exodus 11	Luke 14:1-14	**28**	Job 29	1 Cor. 15:1-29
Exodus 12:1-21	Luke 14:15	**29**	Job 30:1-15	1 Cor. 15:30
Exodus 12:22	Luke 15	**1**	Job 30:16	1 Cor. 16

MARCH

BUT MARY KEPT ALL THESE THINGS AND PONDERED THEM IN HER HEART.

FAMILY			SECRET	
Exodus 12:22	Luke 15	**1**	Job 30	1 Cor. 16
Exodus 13	Luke 16	**2**	Job 31	2 Cor. 1
Exodus 14	Luke 17	**3**	Job 32	2 Cor. 2
Exodus 15	Luke 18	**4**	Job 33	2 Cor. 3
Exodus 16	Luke 19	**5**	Job 34	2 Cor. 4
Exodus 17	Luke 20	**6**	Job 35	2 Cor. 5
Exodus 18	Luke 21	**7**	Job 36	2 Cor. 6
Exodus 19	Luke 22	**8**	Job 37	2 Cor. 7
Exodus 20	Luke 23	**9**	Job 38	2 Cor. 8
Exodus 21	Luke 24	**10**	Job 39	2 Cor. 9
Exodus 22	John 1	**11**	Job 40	2 Cor. 10
Exodus 23	John 2	**12**	Job 41	2 Cor. 11
Exodus 24	John 3	**13**	Job 42	2 Cor. 12
Exodus 25	John 4	**14**	Proverbs 1	2 Cor. 13
Exodus 26	John 5	**15**	Proverbs 2	Galatians 1
Exodus 27	John 6	**16**	Proverbs 3	Galatians 2
Exodus 28	John 7	**17**	Proverbs 4	Galatians 3
Exodus 29	John 8	**18**	Proverbs 5	Galatians 4
Exodus 30	John 9	**19**	Proverbs 6	Galatians 5
Exodus 31	John 10	**20**	Proverbs 7	Galatians 6
Exodus 32	John 11	**21**	Proverbs 8	Ephesians 1
Exodus 33	John 12	**22**	Proverbs 9	Ephesians 2
Exodus 34	John 13	**23**	Proverbs 10	Ephesians 3
Exodus 35	John 14	**24**	Proverbs 11	Ephesians 4
Exodus 36	John 15	**25**	Proverbs 12	Ephesians 5
Exodus 37	John 16	**26**	Proverbs 13	Ephesians 6
Exodus 38	John 17	**27**	Proverbs 14	Phil. 1
Exodus 39	John 18	**28**	Proverbs 15	Phil. 2
Exodus 40	John 19	**29**	Proverbs 16	Phil. 3
Leviticus 1	John 20	**30**	Proverbs 17	Phil. 4
Leviticus 2-3	John 21	**31**	Proverbs 18	Colossians 1

Abbreviations: 1 Cor. – 1 Corinthians; 2 Cor. – 2 Corinthians; Phil. – Philippians

Daily Bread Calendar

APRIL

OH, SEND OUT YOUR LIGHT AND YOUR TRUTH! LET THEM LEAD ME.

FAMILY			SECRET	
Leviticus 4	Psalms 1-2	**1**	Proverbs 19	Colossians 2
Leviticus 5	Psalms 3-4	**2**	Proverbs 20	Colossians 3
Leviticus 6	Psalms 5-6	**3**	Proverbs 21	Colossians 4
Leviticus 7	Psalms 7-8	**4**	Proverbs 22	1 Thess. 1
Leviticus 8	Psalms 9	**5**	Proverbs 23	1 Thess. 2
Leviticus 9	Psalms 10	**6**	Proverbs 24	1 Thess. 3
Leviticus 10	Psalms 11-12	**7**	Proverbs 25	1 Thess. 4
Lev. 11-12	Psalms 13-14	**8**	Proverbs 26	1 Thess. 5
Leviticus 13	Psalms 15-16	**9**	Proverbs 27	2 Thess. 1
Leviticus 14	Psalms 17	**10**	Proverbs 28	2 Thess. 2
Leviticus 15	Psalms 18	**11**	Proverbs 29	2 Thess. 3
Leviticus 16	Psalms 19	**12**	Proverbs 30	1 Timothy 1
Leviticus 17	Psalms 20-21	**13**	Proverbs 31	1 Timothy 2
Leviticus 18	Psalms 22	**14**	Eccles. 1	1 Timothy 3
Leviticus 19	Psalms 23-24	**15**	Eccles. 2	1 Timothy 4
Leviticus 20	Psalms 25	**16**	Eccles. 3	1 Timothy 5
Leviticus 21	Psalms 26-27	**17**	Eccles. 4	1 Timothy 6
Leviticus 22	Psalms 28-29	**18**	Eccles. 5	2 Timothy 1
Leviticus 23	Psalms 30	**19**	Eccles. 6	2 Timothy 2
Leviticus 24	Psalms 31	**20**	Eccles. 7	2 Timothy 3
Leviticus 25	Psalms 32	**21**	Eccles. 8	2 Timothy 4
Leviticus 26	Psalms 33	**22**	Eccles. 9	Titus 1
Leviticus 27	Psalms 34	**23**	Eccles. 10	Titus 2
Numbers 1	Psalms 35	**24**	Eccles. 11	Titus 3
Numbers 2	Psalms 36	**25**	Eccles. 12	Philemon
Numbers 3	Psalms 37	**26**	Song. 1	Hebrews 1
Numbers 4	Psalms 38	**27**	Song. 2	Hebrews 2
Numbers 5	Psalms 39	**28**	Song. 3	Hebrews 3
Numbers 6	Psalms 40-41	**29**	Song. 4	Hebrews 4
Numbers 7	Psalms 42-43	**30**	Song. 5	Hebrews 5

Abbreviations: 1 Thess. – 1 Thessalonians; Lev. – Leviticus;
2 Thess. – 2 Thessalonians; Eccles. – Ecclesiastes;
Song. – Song of Solomon

MAY

FROM CHILDHOOD YOU HAVE KNOWN
THE HOLY SCRIPTURES.

FAMILY			SECRET	
Numbers 8	Psalms 44	**1**	Song. 6	Hebrews 6
Numbers 9	Psalms 45	**2**	Song. 7	Hebrews 7
Numbers 10	Psalms 46-47	**3**	Song. 8	Hebrews 8
Numbers 11	Psalms 48	**4**	Isaiah 1	Hebrews 9
Numb. 12-13	Psalms 49	**5**	Isaiah 2	Hebrews 10
Numbers 14	Psalms 50	**6**	Isaiah 3-4	Hebrews 11
Numbers 15	Psalms 51	**7**	Isaiah 5	Hebrews 12
Numbers 16	Psalms 52-54	**8**	Isaiah 6	Hebrews 13
Numb. 17-18	Psalms 55	**9**	Isaiah 7	James 1
Numbers 19	Psalms 56-57	**10**	Isaiah 8:1-9:7	James 2
Numbers 20	Psalms 58-59	**11**	Isa. 9:8-10:4	James 3
Numbers 21	Psalms 60-61	**12**	Isaiah 10:5	James 4
Numbers 22	Psalms 62-63	**13**	Isaiah 11-12	James 5
Numbers 23	Psalms 64-65	**14**	Isaiah 13	1 Peter 1
Numbers 24	Psalms 66-67	**15**	Isaiah 14	1 Peter 2
Numbers 25	Psalms 68	**16**	Isaiah 15	1 Peter 3
Numbers 26	Psalms 69	**17**	Isaiah 16	1 Peter 4
Numbers 27	Psalms 70-71	**18**	Isaiah 17-18	1 Peter 5
Numbers 28	Psalms 72	**19**	Isaiah 19-20	2 Peter 1
Numbers 29	Psalms 73	**20**	Isaiah 21	2 Peter 2
Numbers 30	Psalms 74	**21**	Isaiah 22	2 Peter 3
Numbers 31	Psalms 75-76	**22**	Isaiah 23	1 John 1
Numbers 32	Psalms 77	**23**	Isaiah 24	1 John 2
Numbers 33	Psalms 78:1-37	**24**	Isaiah 25	1 John 3
Numbers 34	Psalms 78:38	**25**	Isaiah 26	1 John 4
Numbers 35	Psalms 79	**26**	Isaiah 27	1 John 5
Numbers 36	Psalms 80	**27**	Isaiah 28	2 John
Deut. 1	Psalms 81-82	**28**	Isaiah 29	3 John
Deut. 2	Psalms 83-84	**29**	Isaiah 30	Jude
Deut. 3	Psalms 85	**30**	Isaiah 31	Revelation 1
Deut. 4	Psalms 86-87	**31**	Isaiah 32	Revelation 2

Abbreviations: Numb. – Numbers; Deut. – Deuteronomy; Isa. – Isaiah

Daily Bread Calendar

JUNE

BLESSED IS HE WHO READS AND THOSE WHO HEAR.

FAMILY			SECRET	
Deut. 5	Psalms 88	**1**	Isaiah 33	Revelation 3
Deut. 6	Psalms 89	**2**	Isaiah 34	Revelation 4
Deut. 7	Psalms 90	**3**	Isaiah 35	Revelation 5
Deut. 8	Psalms 91	**4**	Isaiah 36	Revelation 6
Deut. 9	Ps. 92-93	**5**	Isaiah 37	Revelation 7
Deut. 10	Psalms 94	**6**	Isaiah 38	Revelation 8
Deut. 11	Ps. 95-96	**7**	Isaiah 39	Revelation 9
Deut. 12	Ps. 97-98	**8**	Isaiah 40	Rev. 10
Deut. 13-14	Ps. 99-101	**9**	Isaiah 41	Rev. 11
Deut. 15	Psalms 102	**10**	Isaiah 42	Rev. 12
Deut. 16	Psalms 103	**11**	Isaiah 43	Rev. 13
Deut. 17	Psalms 104	**12**	Isaiah 44	Rev. 14
Deut. 18	Psalms 105	**13**	Isaiah 45	Rev. 15
Deut. 19	Psalms 106	**14**	Isaiah 46	Rev. 16
Deut. 20	Psalms 107	**15**	Isaiah 47	Rev. 17
Deut. 21	Ps. 108-109	**16**	Isaiah 48	Rev. 18
Deut. 22	Ps. 110-111	**17**	Isaiah 49	Rev. 19
Deut. 23	Ps. 112-113	**18**	Isaiah 50	Rev. 20
Deut. 24	Ps. 114-115	**19**	Isaiah 51	Rev. 21
Deut. 25	Psalms 116	**20**	Isaiah 52	Rev. 22
Deut. 26	Ps. 117-118	**21**	Isaiah 53	Matthew 1
Deut. 27-28:19	119:1-24	**22**	Isaiah 54	Matthew 2
Deut. 28:20	119:25-48	**23**	Isaiah 55	Matthew 3
Deut. 29	119:49-72	**24**	Isaiah 56	Matthew 4
Deut. 30	119:73-96	**25**	Isaiah 57	Matthew 5
Deut. 31	119:97-120	**26**	Isaiah 58	Matthew 6
Deut. 32	119:121-144	**27**	Isaiah 59	Matthew 7
Deut. 33-34	119:145-176	**28**	Isaiah 60	Matthew 8
Joshua 1	Ps. 120-122	**29**	Isaiah 61	Matthew 9
Joshua 2	Ps. 123-125	**30**	Isaiah 62	Matthew 10

Abbreviations: Deut. – Deuteronomy; Ps. – Psalms; Rev. – Revelation

JULY

THEY RECEIVED THE WORD WITH ALL READINESS,
AND SEARCHED THE SCRIPTURES DAILY.

FAMILY			SECRET	
Joshua 3	Ps. 126-128	**1**	Isaiah 63	Matthew 11
Joshua 4	Ps. 129-131	**2**	Isaiah 64	Matthew 12
Joshua 5-6:5	Ps. 132-134	**3**	Isaiah 65	Matthew 13
Joshua 6:6	Ps. 135-136	**4**	Isaiah 66	Matthew 14
Joshua 7	Ps. 137-138	**5**	Jeremiah 1	Matthew 15
Joshua 8	Ps. 139	**6**	Jeremiah 2	Matthew 16
Joshua 9	Ps. 140-141	**7**	Jeremiah 3	Matthew 17
Joshua 10	Ps. 142-143	**8**	Jeremiah 4	Matthew 18
Joshua 11	Ps. 144	**9**	Jeremiah 5	Matthew 19
Joshua 12-13	Ps. 145	**10**	Jeremiah 6	Matthew 20
Joshua 14-15	Ps. 146-147	**11**	Jeremiah 7	Matthew 21
Joshua 16-17	Ps. 148	**12**	Jeremiah 8	Matthew 22
Joshua 18-19	Ps. 149-150	**13**	Jeremiah 9	Matthew 23
Joshua 20-21	Acts 1	**14**	Jeremiah 10	Matthew 24
Joshua 22	Acts 2	**15**	Jeremiah 11	Matthew 25
Joshua 23	Acts 3	**16**	Jeremiah 12	Matthew 26
Joshua 24	Acts 4	**17**	Jeremiah 13	Matthew 27
Judges 1	Acts 5	**18**	Jeremiah 14	Matthew 28
Judges 2	Acts 6	**19**	Jeremiah 15	Mark 1
Judges 3	Acts 7	**20**	Jeremiah 16	Mark 2
Judges 4	Acts 8	**21**	Jeremiah 17	Mark 3
Judges 5	Acts 9	**22**	Jeremiah 18	Mark 4
Judges 6	Acts 10	**23**	Jeremiah 19	Mark 5
Judges 7	Acts 11	**24**	Jeremiah 20	Mark 6
Judges 8	Acts 12	**25**	Jeremiah 21	Mark 7
Judges 9	Acts 13	**26**	Jeremiah 22	Mark 8
Jud. 10-11:11	Acts 14	**27**	Jeremiah 23	Mark 9
Judges 11:12	Acts 15	**28**	Jeremiah 24	Mark 10
Judges 12	Acts 16	**29**	Jeremiah 25	Mark 11
Judges 13	Acts 17	**30**	Jeremiah 26	Mark 12
Judges 14	Acts 18	**31**	Jeremiah 27	Mark 13

Abbreviations: Ps. – Psalms; Jud. – Judges

AUGUST

SPEAK, LORD, FOR YOUR SERVANT HEARS.

FAMILY			SECRET	
Judges 15	Acts 19	**1**	Jeremiah 28	Mark 14
Judges 16	Acts 20	**2**	Jeremiah 29	Mark 15
Judges 17	Acts 21	**3**	Jer. 30-31	Mark 16
Judges 18	Acts 22	**4**	Jeremiah 32	Psalms 1-2
Judges 19	Acts 23	**5**	Jeremiah 33	Psalms 3-4
Judges 20	Acts 24	**6**	Jeremiah 34	Psalms 5-6
Judges 21	Acts 25	**7**	Jeremiah 35	Psalms 7-8
Ruth 1	Acts 26	**8**	Jer. 36-45	Psalms 9
Ruth 2	Acts 27	**9**	Jeremiah 37	Psalms 10
Ruth 3-4	Acts 28	**10**	Jeremiah 38	Psalms 11-12
1 Samuel 1	Romans 1	**11**	Jeremiah 39	Psalms 13-14
1 Samuel 2	Romans 2	**12**	Jeremiah 40	Psalms 15-16
1 Samuel 3	Romans 3	**13**	Jeremiah 41	Psalms 17
1 Samuel 4	Romans 4	**14**	Jeremiah 42	Psalms 18
1 Samuel 5-6	Romans 5	**15**	Jeremiah 43	Psalms 19
1 Samuel 7-8	Romans 6	**16**	Jeremiah 44	Psalms 20-21
1 Samuel 9	Romans 7	**17**	Jeremiah 46	Psalms 22
1 Samuel 10	Romans 8	**18**	Jeremiah 47	Psalms 23-24
1 Samuel 11	Romans 9	**19**	Jeremiah 48	Psalms 25
1 Samuel 12	Romans 10	**20**	Jeremiah 49	Psalms 26-27
1 Samuel 13	Romans 11	**21**	Jeremiah 50	Psalms 28-29
1 Samuel 14	Romans 12	**22**	Jeremiah 51	Psalms 30
1 Samuel 15	Romans 13	**23**	Jeremiah 52	Psalms 31
1 Samuel 16	Romans 14	**24**	Lament. 1	Psalms 32
1 Samuel 17	Romans 15	**25**	Lament. 2	Psalms 33
1 Samuel 18	Romans 16	**26**	Lament. 3	Psalms 34
1 Samuel 19	1 Cor. 1	**27**	Lament. 4	Psalms 35
1 Samuel 20	1 Cor. 2	**28**	Lament. 5	Psalms 36
1 Sam. 21-22	1 Cor. 3	**29**	Ezekiel 1	Psalms 37
1 Samuel 23	1 Cor. 4	**30**	Ezekiel 2	Psalms 38
1 Samuel 24	1 Cor. 5	**31**	Ezekiel 3	Psalms 39

Abbreviations: Jer. – Jeremiah; Lament. – Lamentations;
1 Cor. – 1 Corinthians; 1 Sam. – 1 Samuel

SEPTEMBER

THE LAW OF THE LORD IS PERFECT, CONVERTING THE SOUL.

FAMILY			SECRET	
1 Samuel 25	1 Cor. 6	**1**	Ezekiel 4	Psalms 40-41
1 Samuel 26	1 Cor. 7	**2**	Ezekiel 5	Psalms 42-43
1 Samuel 27	1 Cor. 8	**3**	Ezekiel 6	Psalms 44
1 Samuel 28	1 Cor. 9	**4**	Ezekiel 7	Psalms 45
1 Sam. 29-30	1 Cor. 10	**5**	Ezekiel 8	Psalms 46-47
1 Samuel 31	1 Cor. 11	**6**	Ezekiel 9	Psalms 48
2 Samuel 1	1 Cor. 12	**7**	Ezekiel 10	Psalms 49
2 Samuel 2	1 Cor. 13	**8**	Ezekiel 11	Psalms 50
2 Samuel 3	1 Cor. 14	**9**	Ezekiel 12	Psalms 51
2 Samuel 4-5	1 Cor. 15	**10**	Ezekiel 13	Psalms 52-54
2 Samuel 6	1 Cor. 16	**11**	Ezekiel 14	Psalms 55
2 Samuel 7	2 Cor. 1	**12**	Ezekiel 15	Psalms 56-57
2 Samuel 8-9	2 Cor. 2	**13**	Ezekiel 16	Psalms 58-59
2 Samuel 10	2 Cor. 3	**14**	Ezekiel 17	Psalms 60-61
2 Samuel 11	2 Cor. 4	**15**	Ezekiel 18	Psalms 62-63
2 Samuel 12	2 Cor. 5	**16**	Ezekiel 19	Psalms 64-65
2 Samuel 13	2 Cor. 6	**17**	Ezekiel 20	Psalms 66-67
2 Samuel 14	2 Cor. 7	**18**	Ezekiel 21	Psalms 68
2 Samuel 15	2 Cor. 8	**19**	Ezekiel 22	Psalms 69
2 Samuel 16	2 Cor. 9	**20**	Ezekiel 23	Psalms 70-71
2 Samuel 17	2 Cor. 10	**21**	Ezekiel 24	Psalms 72
2 Samuel 18	2 Cor. 11	**22**	Ezekiel 25	Psalms 73
2 Samuel 19	2 Cor. 12	**23**	Ezekiel 26	Psalms 74
2 Samuel 20	2 Cor. 13	**24**	Ezekiel 27	Psalms 75-76
2 Samuel 21	Galatians 1	**25**	Ezekiel 28	Psalms 77
2 Samuel 22	Galatians 2	**26**	Ezekiel 29	Psalms 78:1-37
2 Samuel 23	Galatians 3	**27**	Ezekiel 30	Psalms 78:38
2 Samuel 24	Galatians 4	**28**	Ezekiel 31	Psalms 79
1 Kings 1	Galatians 5	**29**	Ezekiel 32	Psalms 80
1 Kings 2	Galatians 6	**30**	Ezekiel 33	Psalms 81-82

Abbreviations: 1 Cor. – 1 Corinthians; 2 Cor. – 2 Corinthians;
1 Sam. – 1 Samuel

Daily Bread Calendar

OCTOBER

OH HOW I LOVE YOUR LAW! IT IS MY MEDITATION ALL THE DAY.

FAMILY			SECRET	
1 Kings 3	Ephesians 1	**1**	Ezekiel 34	Psalms 83-84
1 Kings 4-5	Ephesians 2	**2**	Ezekiel 35	Psalms 85
1 Kings 6	Ephesians 3	**3**	Ezekiel 36	Psalms 86
1 Kings 7	Ephesians 4	**4**	Ezekiel 37	Psalm 87-88
1 Kings 8	Ephesians 5	**5**	Ezekiel 38	Psalms 89
1 Kings 9	Ephesians 6	**6**	Ezekiel 39	Psalms 90
1 Kings 10	Phil. 1	**7**	Ezekiel 40	Psalms 91
1 Kings 11	Phil. 2	**8**	Ezekiel 41	Ps. 92-93
1 Kings 12	Phil. 3	**9**	Ezekiel 42	Psalms 94
1 Kings 13	Phil. 4	**10**	Ezekiel 43	Ps. 95-96
1 Kings 14	Colossians 1	**11**	Ezekiel 44	Ps. 97-98
1 Kings 15	Colossians 2	**12**	Ezekiel 45	Ps. 99-101
1 Kings 16	Colossians 3	**13**	Ezekiel 46	Psalms 102
1 Kings 17	Colossians 4	**14**	Ezekiel 47	Psalms 103
1 Kings 18	1 Thess. 1	**15**	Ezekiel 48	Psalms 104
1 Kings 19	1 Thess. 2	**16**	Daniel 1	Psalms 105
1 Kings 20	1 Thess. 3	**17**	Daniel 2	Psalms 106
1 Kings 21	1 Thess. 4	**18**	Daniel 3	Psalms 107
1 Kings 22	1 Thess. 5	**19**	Daniel 4	Ps. 108-109
2 Kings 1	2 Thess. 1	**20**	Daniel 5	Ps. 110-111
2 Kings 2	2 Thess. 2	**21**	Daniel 6	Ps. 112-113
2 Kings 3	2 Thess. 3	**22**	Daniel 7	Ps. 114-115
2 Kings 4	1 Timothy 1	**23**	Daniel 8	Psalms 116
2 Kings 5	1 Timothy 2	**24**	Daniel 9	Ps. 117-118
2 Kings 6	1 Timothy 3	**25**	Daniel 10	Ps. 119:1-24
2 Kings 7	1 Timothy 4	**26**	Daniel 11	Ps. 119:25-48
2 Kings 8	1 Timothy 5	**27**	Daniel 12	Ps. 119:49-72
2 Kings 9	1 Timothy 6	**28**	Hosea 1	Ps. 119:73-96
2 Kings 10	2 Timothy 1	**29**	Hosea 2	Ps. 119:97-120
2 Kings 11-12	2 Timothy 2	**30**	Hosea 3-4	Ps. 119:121-144
2 Kings 13	2 Timothy 3	**31**	Hosea 5-6	Ps. 119:145-176

Abbreviations: Phil. – Philippians; Ps. – Psalms; 1 Thess. – 1 Thessalonians; 2 Thess. – 2 Thessalonians

NOVEMBER

AS NEWBORN BABES, DESIRE THE PURE MILK OF THE WORD,
THAT YOU MAY GROW THEREBY.

FAMILY			SECRET	
2 Kings 14	2 Timothy 4	**1**	Hosea 7	Ps. 120-122
2 Kings 15	Titus 1	**2**	Hosea 8	Ps. 123-125
2 Kings 16	Titus 2	**3**	Hosea 9	Ps. 126-128
2 Kings 17	Titus 3	**4**	Hosea 10	Ps. 129-131
2 Kings 18	Philemon	**5**	Hosea 11	Ps. 132-134
2 Kings 19	Hebrews 1	**6**	Hosea 12	Ps. 135-136
2 Kings 20	Hebrews 2	**7**	Hosea 13	Ps. 137-138
2 Kings 21	Hebrews 3	**8**	Hosea 14	Psalms 139
2 Kings 22	Hebrews 4	**9**	Joel 1	Ps. 140-141
2 Kings 23	Hebrews 5	**10**	Joel 2	Psalms 142
2 Kings 24	Hebrews 6	**11**	Joel 3	Psalms 143
2 Kings 25	Hebrews 7	**12**	Amos 1	Psalms 144
1 Chron. 1-2	Hebrews 8	**13**	Amos 2	Psalms 145
1 Chron. 3-4	Hebrews 9	**14**	Amos 3	Ps. 146-147
1 Chron. 5-6	Hebrews 10	**15**	Amos 4	Ps. 148-150
1 Chron. 7-8	Hebrews 11	**16**	Amos 5	Luke 1:1-38
1 Chron. 9-10	Hebrews 12	**17**	Amos 6	Luke 1:39
1 Chron. 11-12	Hebrews 13	**18**	Amos 7	Luke 2
1 Chron. 13-14	James 1	**19**	Amos 8	Luke 3
1 Chron. 15	James 2	**20**	Amos 9	Luke 4
1 Chron. 16	James 3	**21**	Obadiah	Luke 5
1 Chron. 17	James 4	**22**	Jonah 1	Luke 6
1 Chron. 18	James 5	**23**	Jonah 2	Luke 7
1 Chron. 19-20	1 Peter 1	**24**	Jonah 3	Luke 8
1 Chron. 21	1 Peter 2	**25**	Jonah 4	Luke 9
1 Chron. 22	1 Peter 3	**26**	Micah 1	Luke 10
1 Chron. 23	1 Peter 4	**27**	Micah 2	Luke 11
1 Chron. 24-25	1 Peter 5	**28**	Micah 3	Luke 12
1 Chron. 26-27	2 Peter 1	**29**	Micah 4	Luke 13
1 Chron. 28	2 Peter 2	**30**	Micah 5	Luke 14

Abbreviations: Ps. – Psalms; 1 Chron. – 1 Chronicles

DECEMBER

THE LAW OF HIS GOD IS IN HIS HEART; NONE OF HIS STEPS SHALL SLIDE.

FAMILY			SECRET	
1 Chron. 29	2 Peter 3	**1**	Micah 6	Luke 15
2 Chron. 1	1 John 1	**2**	Micah 7	Luke 16
2 Chron. 2	1 John 2	**3**	Nahum 1	Luke 17
2 Chron. 3-4	1 John 3	**4**	Nahum 2	Luke 18
2 Chron. 5-6:11	1 John 4	**5**	Nahum 3	Luke 19
2 Chron. 6:12	1 John 5	**6**	Hab. 1	Luke 20
2 Chron. 7	2 John	**7**	Hab. 2	Luke 21
2 Chron. 8	3 John	**8**	Hab. 3	Luke 22
2 Chron. 9	Jude	**9**	Zephaniah 1	Luke 23
2 Chron. 10	Revelation 1	**10**	Zephaniah 2	Luke 24
2 Chron. 11-12	Revelation 2	**11**	Zephaniah 3	John 1
2 Chron. 13	Revelation 3	**12**	Haggai 1	John 2
2 Chron. 14-15	Revelation 4	**13**	Haggai 2	John 3
2 Chron. 16	Revelation 5	**14**	Zechariah 1	John 4
2 Chron. 17	Revelation 6	**15**	Zechariah 2	John 5
2 Chron. 18	Revelation 7	**16**	Zechariah 3	John 6
2 Chron. 19-20	Revelation 8	**17**	Zechariah 4	John 7
2 Chron. 21	Revelation 9	**18**	Zechariah 5	John 8
2 Chron. 22-23	Rev. 10	**19**	Zechariah 6	John 9
2 Chron.24	Rev. 11	**20**	Zechariah 7	John 10
2 Chron. 25	Rev. 12	**21**	Zechariah 8	John 11
2 Chron. 26	Rev. 13	**22**	Zechariah 9	John 12
2 Chron. 27-28	Rev. 14	**23**	Zechariah 10	John 13
2 Chron. 29	Rev. 15	**24**	Zechariah 11	John 14
2 Chron. 30	Rev. 16	**25**	Zechariah 12	John 15
2 Chron. 31	Rev. 17	**26**	Zechariah 13	John 16
2 Chron. 33	Rev. 18	**27**	Zechariah 14	John 17
2 Chron. 34	Rev. 19	**28**	Malachi 1	John 18
2 Chron. 35	Rev. 20	**29**	Malachi 2	John 19
2 Chron. 36	Rev. 21	**30**	Malachi 3	John 20
2 Chron. 37	Rev. 22	**31**	Malachi 4	John 21

Abbreviations: 1 Chron. – 1 Chronicles; 2 Chron. – 2 Chronicles; Hab. – Habakkuk; Rev. – Revelation

5.

1689 LONDON BAPTIST CONFESSION INTRODUCTION & INSTRUCTION

THE 1689 LONDON BAPTIST CONFESSION, also known as the Second London Baptist Confession, is an excellent systematic theology. In other words, it presents an excellent systematic explanation of the things we believe concerning God. Charles Haddon Spurgeon said this about the 1689 London Baptist Confession, a creed that defined his basic beliefs and that of his congregation at the Metropolitan Tabernacle:

> "This ancient document is the most excellent epitome of the things most surely believed among us. It is not issued as an authoritative rule or code of faith, whereby you may be fettered, but as a means of edification in righteousness. It is an excellent, though not inspired, expression of the teaching of those Holy Scriptures by which all confessions are to be measured. We hold to the humbling truths of God's sovereign grace in the salvation of lost sinners. Salvation is through Christ alone and by faith alone."

Even if you, your family, or the church you attend as a member, have a different confession of faith than the 1689 London Baptist Confession, I believe that you will still benefit greatly from the use of this confession and its Scripture proofs. Although the church I presently pastor, Sovereign Grace Baptist Church, in Anniston, Alabama, was formed as a local Baptist Church standing in agreement with the 1646 London Baptist Confession, and also in general agreement with the first American Baptist Confession, called the Philadelphia Baptist Confession of 1742, I stand in agreement with them in their agreement to those confessions; and the congregation, also, though it is not written as any creed within their constitution, have no objections to my stance in using the second London Baptist Confession as a defining creed.

So how can we incorporate the 1689 London Baptist Confession into the family devotion for the mutual edification of its members?

First, it could be read in the evenings prior to, or after, the family Bible reading from the Daily Bread Scripture portions for that day; just as the catechism is read as a supplement to the devotional Scripture portions in the morning. There are thirty-two chapters in the 1689 Confession so you might want to combine one of any of the following two-chapter combinations on the day of its appropriate reading: chapters 9 and 10; chapters 24 and 25; chapters 28 and 29; or chapters 31 and 32. During months with only 30 days, use any two of the two-chapter combinations listed. In February, use all four two-chapter combinations; except in a leap year, when, of course, you would only use three.

You might decide that you would rather just read one chapter per evening until you've read through the confession together as a family once, or even several times. It is entirely up to you. In that case, you'll want to refer to the last chapter of this family devotional for some helpful suggestions.

6.

SECOND LONDON BAPTIST CONFESSION OF FAITH — 1677/1689

I. THE HOLY SCRIPTURES

1. THE HOLY SCRIPTURE is the only sufficient, certain, and infallible standard of all saving knowledge, faith, and obedience. Although the light of nature and the works of creation and providence clearly show the goodness, wisdom, and power of God so much that man is left without any excuse, they are not sufficient to provide that knowledge of God and His will which is necessary for salvation. Therefore, it pleased the Lord at various times and in different ways to reveal Himself, and to declare His will unto His church; and afterward for the better preservation and distribution of the truth, and for the more definite establishment and comfort of the church, protecting it against the corruption of the flesh and the wicked hatred of Satan and the world, it pleased the Lord to commit His revealed Truth completely to writing. Therefore, the Holy Scriptures are most necessary, those former ways of God's revealing His will to His people having now ceased.[1]

2. Under the name of Holy Scripture, the written Word of God, or the Holy Bible, the Old and New Testaments are now contained within all of the following books:

Of the Old Testament: Genesis, Exodus, Leviticus, Numbers, Deuteronomy, Joshua, Judges, Ruth, 1 Samuel, 2 Samuel, 1 Kings, 2 Kings, 1 Chronicles, 2 Chronicles, Ezra, Nehemiah, Esther, Job, Psalms, Proverbs,

Ecclesiastes, Song of Solomon, Isaiah, Jeremiah, Lamentations, Ezekiel, Daniel, Hosea, Joel, Amos, Obadiah, Jonah, Micah, Nahum, Habakkuk, Zephaniah, Haggai, Zechariah, Malachi

Of the New Testament: Matthew, Mark, Luke, John, Acts, Romans, 1 Corinthians, 2 Corinthians, Galatians, Ephesians, Philippians, Colossians, 1 Thessalonians, 2 Thessalonians, 1 Timothy, 2 Timothy, Titus, Philemon, Hebrews, James, 1 Peter, 2 Peter, 1 John, 2 John, 3 John, Jude, Revelation

All of these books are given by the inspiration of God to be the standard of faith and life.[2]

3. The books commonly called Apocrypha are not divinely inspired and are not part of the canon (or standard) of the Scripture; therefore, they have no authority to the church of God, nor are they to be approved of or made use of any differently than other human writings.[3]

4. The authority of the Holy Scripture, for which it ought to be believed, does not depend upon the testimony of any man or church, but depends wholly and completely upon God, its Author, who is Truth itself. Therefore, it is to be received because it is the Word of God.[4]

5. We may be moved and persuaded by the testimony of the people of God to gain a high and reverent regard for the Holy Scriptures. We may be affected by the nature of the Scriptures in the same way— the heavenliness of the contents, the value and effectiveness of the doctrine, the majesty of the style, the agreement of all its parts, the scope of the whole (which is to give all glory to God), the full disclosure it makes of the only way of man's salvation, together with many other unique excellencies and entire perfections. By all the evidence, the Scripture more than proves itself to be the Word of God. Yet, this notwithstanding, our full persuasion and assurance of the infallible truth of Scripture and its divine authority, is from the inward work of the Holy Spirit bearing witness by the Word, and with the Word, in our hearts.[5]

6. The whole counsel of God concerning all things necessary for His own glory, man's salvation, faith and life, is either

specifically set down or essentially contained in the Holy Scripture, unto which nothing at any time is to be added, whether by new revelation of the Spirit, or traditions of men. Nevertheless, we acknowledge the inward illumination of the Spirit of God to be necessary for the saving understanding of such things as are revealed in the Word. There are some circumstances concerning the worship of God, and government of the church, common to human actions and societies, which are to be ordered by the light of nature, Christian wisdom, and careful judgment, according to the general rules of the Word, which are always to be observed.[6]

7. All things in Scripture are not equally plain in themselves, nor equally clear to everyone; yet, those things which are necessary to be known, believed and observed for salvation, are so clearly put forth and revealed in some place of Scripture or another, that not only the educated person, but also the uneducated, may gain a sufficient understanding of them by the proper use of ordinary means.[7]

8. The Old Testament in Hebrew, which was the native language of the people of God long ago, and the New Testament in Greek, which at the time of its writing was the most widely used language in the civilized nations, were immediately inspired by God, and were kept pure throughout the ages by His remarkable care and providence. Therefore, they are authentic, so that in all debates concerning religion, the church is to appeal to them as final. Yet, because these original languages are not known to all the people of God who have a right to the Scriptures, and an interest in them, and because they are commanded to read them and search them in the fear of God, they are to be translated into the ordinary language of every nation into which the Scriptures come, so that, with the Word of God living richly in all people, they may worship Him in an acceptable manner, and through patience and comfort of the Scriptures, they may have hope.[8]

9. The infallible standard for the interpretation of Scripture is the Scripture itself. Therefore, whenever there is a question about the true and full sense of any Scripture, which is not many but one, it must be searched by other passages that speak more clearly.[9]

10. The supreme judge, by which all debates concerning religion are to be determined, and by which must be examined all decrees of councils, opinions of ancient writers, and doctrines of

men and private spirits can be no other than the Holy Scripture, delivered by the Spirit. And in the verdict of Scripture we are to rest, for it is in Scripture, delivered by the Spirit, that our faith is finally resolved.[10]

II. GOD & THE HOLY TRINITY

1. THE LORD OUR GOD is the one and only living and true God. His existence is in and of Himself, infinite in being and perfection. His essence cannot be completely understood by any but Himself. He is a most pure spirit, invisible, without body, parts, or passions; who alone has immortality, dwelling in the light that no man can approach. He is immutable, immense, eternal, incomprehensible, almighty, in every way infinite, most holy, most wise, most free, and most absolute. He works all things according to the counsel of His own absolute, unchallengeable and most righteous will for His own glory. He is most loving, gracious, merciful, longsuffering, abundant in goodness and truth, forgiving iniquity, transgression, and sin. He is the One who rewards those that diligently seek Him; and at the same time, He is most just and terrible in His judgments, hating all sin, and who will by no means clear the guilty.[11]

2. God is unique in being all-sufficient, both in Himself and to Himself, having all life, glory, goodness, blessedness, in and of Himself. God does not stand in need of any creature that He has made, nor does He derive any glory from them. On the contrary, it is God who manifests His own glory in them, to them, and upon them. He is the only fountain of all being; of whom, through whom, and to whom all things exist and move. He has complete sovereign power and authority over all creatures, to do through them, for them, or to them whatever He pleases. In His sight all things are open and manifest. His knowledge is infinite, infallible, and not dependent upon the creature. Therefore, nothing is for Him contingent or uncertain. He is most holy in all His counsels, in all His works, and in all His commands; to Him is due from angels and men, whatsoever worship, service, or obedience, as creatures they owe unto the Creator, and whatever He is further

pleased to require of them.[12]

3. In this divine and infinite Being there are three real Persons, the Father, the Word (or Son), and Holy Spirit, of one substance, power, and eternity, each having the whole divine essence, yet the essence is undivided: the Father was not derived from any being; neither was He begotten nor did He come forth from any other being; the Son is eternally begotten of the Father; the Holy Spirit proceeds from the Father and the Son. All three are infinite, without beginning, and is therefore only one God, who is not divided in nature and being, but distinguished by several peculiar relative properties and personal relations. This doctrine of the Trinity is the foundation of our entire communion with God, and comfortable dependence on Him.[13]

III. GOD'S DECREE

1. GOD HAS DECREED IN HIMSELF, from all eternity, by the most wise and holy counsel of His own will, freely and unchangeably, all things, whatsoever comes to pass; yet, this is done in such a way that God is neither the author or origin of sin nor has fellowship with any in the committing of sin; nor is violence offered to the will of the creature, nor is the liberty or contingency of second causes taken away, but rather established. In all this God's wisdom is displayed in arranging all things, and power and faithfulness in accomplishing His decree.[14]

2. Although God knows everything that may or can come to pass, upon all imaginable conditions, yet He has not decreed anything because He foresaw it in the future, or because it would come to pass upon certain conditions.[15]

3. By the decree of God, for the manifestation of His glory, some men and angels are predestined, or foreordained, to eternal life through Jesus Christ, to the praise of His glorious grace; others are left to act in their sin to their just condemnation, to the praise of His glorious justice.[16]

4. These angels and men that are predestined and foreordained are fundamentally and unchangeably designed, and the number of them that are predestined and foreordained are so

certain and definite, that it cannot be either increased or diminished.[17]

5. Those of mankind who are predestined to life have been chosen by God before the foundation of the world was laid, in accordance with His eternal and unchallengeable purpose and the secret counsel and good pleasure of His will. God chose them in Christ for everlasting glory, solely out of His free grace and love, without anything in the creature as a condition or cause to move Him to choose.[18]

6. As God has appointed the elect unto glory, so, by the eternal and completely free intention of His will, He has foreordained all the means to carry it out. Accordingly, Christ redeems those who are elected, being fallen in Adam. They are effectually called unto faith in Christ by His Spirit working in due season. They are justified, adopted, sanctified; and kept by His power through faith unto salvation; and only the elect redeemed by Christ are effectually called, justified, adopted, sanctified, and saved and no others.[19]

7. The doctrine of this high mystery of predestination is to be handled with special care and wise discretion, in order that men who are heeding the will of God revealed in His Word, and who are yielding obedience to it, may from the certainty of their effectual vocation, be assured of their eternal election. Therefore, this doctrine shall provide cause for praise, reverence, and admiration of God, and will also provide cause for humility, diligence, and abundant consolation to all who sincerely obey the Gospel.[20]

IV. CREATION

1. IN THE BEGINNING it pleased God the Father, Son, and Holy Spirit, for the manifestation of the glory of His eternal power, wisdom, and goodness, to create the world, and all things in it, whether visible or invisible, in the space of six days, and all very good.[21]

2. After God had made all other creatures, He created man, male and female, with reasoning and immortal souls, making

them suitable unto that life to God for which they were created. They were made after the image of God, in knowledge, righteousness, and true holiness; having the law of God written in their hearts, and power to fulfill it, and yet under a possibility of transgressing, being left to the liberty of their own will, which was subject to change.[22]

3. Besides the law written in their hearts, they received a command not to eat of the tree of the knowledge of good and evil. While they kept this command, they were happy in their communion with God, and had dominion over all other creatures.[23]

V. DIVINE PROVIDENCE

1. GOD THE GOOD CREATOR of all things, in His infinite power and wisdom, upholds, directs, disposes, and governs all creatures and things, from the greatest to the least, by His most wise and holy providence, to the purpose for which they were created, according to His infallible foreknowledge, and the free and immutable counsel of His own will; to the praise of the glory of His wisdom, power, justice, infinite goodness, and mercy.[24]

2. Although in relation to the foreknowledge and decree of God, who is the first cause, all things come to pass immutably and infallibly; so that nothing happens to anyone by chance, or without His providence; yet by His providence, He orders events to occur according to the nature of second causes; either necessarily, freely, or contingently.[25]

3. God, in His ordinary providence makes use of means, yet is free to work without, above, and against them at His pleasure.[26]

4. The almighty power, unsearchable wisdom, and infinite goodness of God, so far manifest themselves in His providence that His decisive, conclusive, and fixed counsel extends itself even to the first fall, and all other sinful actions both of angels and men. This is not merely a simple permission, but by form of permission in which He included the most wise and powerful limitations, and other means of restricting and controlling sin. These various limitations have been designed by God to bring about His most

holy purposes; yet, in all these dealings, the sinfulness of both angels and men comes only from them and not from God, who is altogether holy and righteous, and can never be the origin, author, or approver of sin.[27]

5. The most wise, righteous, and gracious God often leaves His own children to various temptations and to the corruptions of their own hearts for a period of time, in order to discipline them for the sins which they have committed, or to show them the hidden strength of corruption and deceitfulness still within their hearts, so that they may be humbled and be aroused to a closer and constant dependence upon God for their support; additionally, this is done so that they may be made more watchful against future occasions of sin, as well as for other just and holy ends. So whatever happens to any of His elect is by His appointment, for His glory, and their good.[28]

6. As God, the righteous Judge, blinds and hardens those wicked and ungodly men for former sin, He not only withholds His grace from them, by which they might have been enlightened in their understanding and affected in their hearts, but sometimes He also withdraws the gifts which they had, and exposes them to certain things which their corrupt state will conveniently use as an opportunity to sin. God gives them over to their own lusts, the temptations of the world, and the power of Satan, so that eventually they harden themselves under the influence that God uses for the softening of others.[29]

7. As the providence of God in general reaches to all creatures, so in a more special manner it takes care of His church, and governs all things for their good.[30]

VI. THE FALL OF MAN, SIN, & PUNISHMENT

1. ALTHOUGH GOD created man upright and perfect, and gave him a righteous law, which secured life for him while he kept it, and threatened him with death upon breaking it, yet man did not abide long in this honorable circumstance; Satan using the subtlety of the serpent to deceive Eve, seduced Adam by her, and without any compulsion, Adam willfully transgressed the law of

their creation and the command given to them by eating the forbidden fruit. According to His wise and holy counsel, God was pleased to permit this act, having purposed to ordain it for His own glory.[31]

2. By this sin our first parents fell from their original righteousness and communion with God, and we fell in them; and from this, death came upon all: all becoming dead in sin, and wholly defiled in all the faculties and parts of soul and body.[32]

3. By God's divine appointment they were the root cause, standing in the place of all mankind, the guilt of the sin was imputed and corrupted nature passed on to all their descendents by ordinary generation; their descendants were therefore conceived in sin, and by nature the children of wrath, the servants of sin, the subjects of death, and all other miseries, spiritual, temporal, and eternal, unless the Lord Jesus set them free.[33]

4. All actual transgressions proceed from this original corruption, by which we are utterly indisposed, disabled, and made opposite to all good, and utterly and completely inclined to all evil.[34]

5. During this life, the corruption of nature remains in those who are regenerated; and although it is pardoned and mortified through Christ, yet this corrupt nature and all its motions are truly and properly sinful.[35]

VII. GOD'S COVENANT

1. THE DISTANCE between God and the creature is so enormous, that although reasonable creatures owe obedience to Him as their Creator, yet they could never have reached the reward of life except by some voluntary condescension on God's part, and this He has been pleased to express by way of a covenant.[36]

2. Moreover, it pleased the Lord to make a covenant of grace with fallen man after having brought himself under the curse of the law. In this covenant God freely offers to sinners life and salvation by Jesus Christ, requiring from them faith in Him, that they may be saved; and promising to give to all who are appointed

to eternal life, His Holy Spirit to make them willing and able to believe.[37]

3. This covenant is revealed in the Gospel; first of all to Adam in the promise of salvation by the Seed of the woman, and afterwards by further steps until the full revelation of the Gospel became completed in the New Testament. The covenant of salvation is founded upon an eternal covenant transaction between the Father and the Son about the redemption of the elect. It is solely by the grace of this covenant that all the descendents of fallen Adam who have ever been saved have obtained life and blessed immortality, because man is now utterly incapable of gaining acceptance with God on the terms by which Adam stood in his state of innocence.[38]

VIII. CHRIST THE MEDIATOR

1. IN GOD'S ETERNAL PURPOSE it pleased Him to choose and ordain the Lord Jesus, His only begotten Son, according to the covenant made between both of them, to be the Mediator between God and man; to be Prophet, Priest, and King, the Head and Savior of His church, the Heir of all things, and Judge of the world. From all eternity, God gave to the Lord Jesus a people to be His seed. In time, these people would be redeemed, called, justified, sanctified, and glorified by the Lord Jesus.[39]

2. The Son of God, the second Person in the Holy Trinity, being true and eternal God, the brightness of the Father's glory, of the same substance and equal with Him, made the world, and upholds and governs all things He has made. When the fullness of time had come, the Son had taken upon Himself man's nature, with all the essential properties and common infirmities of man's nature, with the exception of sin. The Son was conceived by the Holy Spirit in the womb of the Virgin Mary, the Holy Spirit coming down upon her and the power of the Most High overshadowing her, so that He was born to a woman from the tribe of Judah, a descendent of Abraham and David, according to the Scriptures. Therefore, two whole, perfect, and distinct natures were inseparably joined together in one Person, without conversion,

composition, or confusion; so that the Lord Jesus Christ is truly God and truly man, yet He is one Christ, the only Mediator between God and man.[40]

3. Once in the Person of the Son, and in His human nature thus united to the divine, the Lord Jesus was sanctified and anointed with the Holy Spirit above measure, having in Him all the treasures of wisdom and knowledge. It pleased the Father that all the fullness of God should dwell in Him, so that being holy, harmless, undefiled, and full of grace and truth, He might be thoroughly furnished to execute the office of Mediator and Surety; a position and duty that He did not take upon Himself, but was called to perform by His Father, who also put all power and judgment in His hand, and gave Him commandment to carry out the same.[41]

4. The Lord Jesus undertook this office of Mediator and Surety most willingly. To discharge it, He was made under the law and perfectly fulfilled the law, and underwent the punishment due to us, which we should have received and suffered. He was made sin and a curse for us, enduring the most grievous sorrows in His soul, and most painful sufferings in His body. He was crucified, and died, and remained in the state of the dead, yet His body did not undergo any decomposition. On the third day He arose from the dead with the same body in which He suffered, and with that same body, He also ascended into heaven, and there sits at the right hand of His Father making intercession; and in that same body, He shall return to judge men and angels at the end of the world.[42]

5. By His perfect obedience and sacrifice of Himself, which the Lord Jesus offered up unto God through the eternal Spirit, has fully satisfied the justice of God, obtain reconciliation, and has purchased an everlasting inheritance in the kingdom of heaven for all those whom the Father has given unto Him.[43]

6. Although the price of redemption was not actually paid by Christ until after His incarnation, the virtue, value, effectiveness, and benefit arising from His payment were communicated to the elect in all ages from the beginning of the world, in and by those promises, types, and sacrifices in which He was revealed and signified to be the Seed which should bruise the serpent's head; and also the Lamb slain from the foundation of the world, being

the same yesterday, and today and forever.[44]

7. In the work of mediation, Christ acts according to both natures, human and divine, each nature doing what is proper to itself; yet because of the unity of His person, that which is proper to one nature is, sometimes in Scripture, attributed to the person named by the other nature.[45]

8. To all those for whom Christ has obtained eternal redemption, He certainly and effectually applies and communicates this redemption, making intercession for them, uniting them to Himself by His Spirit, revealing to them the mystery of salvation in His Word and by His Word. Christ persuades them to believe and obey, governing their hearts by His Word and Spirit, and overcoming all their enemies by His almighty power and wisdom. This is accomplished in such manner and in such a way as are most consistent with His wonderful and unsearchable distribution; and all of this by free and absolute grace, without any condition foreseen in them to obtain it.[46]

9. This office of Mediator between God and man is only proper to Christ, who is the Prophet, Priest, and King of the church of God. This office may not be transferred to any other, either in whole or in part.[47]

10. This number and order of offices is essential. Because of our ignorance, we need His prophetic office. Because of our separation from God and the imperfection of the best of our services, we need His priestly office to reconcile us and present us acceptable unto God. Because of our opposition, reluctance, and utter inability to return to God, and for our rescue and security from our spiritual adversaries, we need His kingly office to convince, subdue, draw, uphold, deliver, and preserve us until we reach His heavenly kingdom.[48]

IX. FREE WILL

1. GOD HAS FURNISHED the will of man with that natural liberty and the power to choose and act upon his choice. This free will is neither forced, nor destined by any necessity of nature to do good or evil.[49]

2. In his state of innocence, man had freedom and power to will good, to do good, and through his free will, be well-pleasing to God; but he was unstable, so that he might fall from this condition.[50]

3. By his fall into a state of sin, man has completely lost all ability of will to perform any spiritual good accompanying salvation. As a natural man, he is altogether opposed to spiritual good, and dead in sin, unable by his own strength to convert himself, or to prepare himself for conversion.[51]

4. When God converts a sinner, and translates him into the state of grace, He frees him from his natural bondage under sin, and by His grace alone enables him freely to will and to do that which is spiritually good. But because of his remaining corruptions, he does not only or perfectly will that which is good, but also wills that which is evil.[52]

5. This will of man will only be made perfectly, absolutely, and unchangeably free to will and to do good in the state of glory.[53]

X. EFFECTUAL CALLING

1. THOSE WHOM GOD has predestined to life by His Word and Spirit, He is pleased in His appointed and accepted time to effectually call out of that state of sin and death which they are in by nature, to grace and salvation by Jesus Christ. He enlightens their minds spiritually with good sense to understand the things of God, taking away their heart of stone, and giving to them a heart of flesh. He renews their wills and, by His almighty power, causes them to desire and pursue that which is good. He effectually draws them to Jesus Christ, yet, He does so in such a way that they come absolutely freely, being made willing by His grace.[54]

2. This effectual call is by God's free and special grace alone, not from anything at all foreseen in man, nor from any power or agency in the creature, which is completely inactive in the matter. Man is dead in sins and trespasses until revived and renewed by the Holy Spirit. By this, he is enabled to answer this call, and to embrace the grace offered and communicated by it. This enabling is accomplished by the same power that raised up Christ from the

dead.[55]

3. Elect infants dying in infancy are regenerated and saved by Christ through the Spirit, as the Spirit works when, where, and how He pleases. The same is also true of all elect persons, who are incapable of being outwardly called by the ministry of the Word.[56]

4. Others not elected, although they may be called by the ministry of the Word and may have some common operations of the Spirit, will not and cannot truly come to Christ because they are not effectually drawn by the Father; therefore they cannot be saved. This is truer still concerning men that do not embrace the Christian religion: that they cannot be saved, regardless of how diligent they may be to structure their lives according to the light of nature and the requirements of that religion they profess.[57]

XI. JUSTIFICATION

1. THOSE WHOM GOD effectually calls He also freely justifies, not by pouring righteousness into them, but by pardoning their sins, and by accounting and accepting them as righteous; not for anything produced in them, or done by them, but for Christ's sake alone. They are not justified because God considers their righteousness as coming from their faith itself, the act of believing, or any other evangelical obedience to them. They are justified completely and solely because God imputes to them Christ's righteousness. God imputes to them Christ's active obedience unto the whole law, and His passive obedience in death. They receive Christ's righteousness by faith and rest on Him. They do not possess or produce this faith themselves for it is the gift of God.[58]

2. Faith that receives and depends on Christ and His righteousness is the only instrument of justification; yet it is not alone in the person justified, but is always accompanied by all other saving graces. It is not a dead faith, but works by love.[59]

3. By His obedience and death, Christ fully paid the debt of all those that are justified, and by the sacrifice of Himself in the blood of His cross, underwent instead of them, the penalty due to them, and therefore, made a proper, real, and full satisfaction to God's justice on their behalf. Yet, because He was given by the Father for

them, and because His obedience and satisfaction was accepted instead of theirs (and both freely, not because of anything in them), therefore, they are justified solely and entirely by free grace, so that both the exact justice and the rich grace of God might be glorified in the justification of sinners.[60]

4. From all eternity God decreed to justify all the elect; Christ died for their sins in the fullness of time, and rose again for their justification. Nevertheless, they are not personally justified until the Holy Spirit actually applies Christ to them in due time.[61]

5. God continues to forgive the sins of those that are justified, and although they can never fall from the state of justification, yet because of their sins, they may fall under God's fatherly displeasure. In that condition they will not usually have the light of His countenance restored to them until they humble themselves, confess their sins, beg for pardon, and renew their faith and repentance.[62]

6. In all these respects, the justification of believers during the Old Testament period was exactly the same as the justification of believers under the New Testament.[63]

XII. ADOPTION

GOD HAS GRANTED permission that all of those that are justified in Christ, His only Son, and for His sake, shall partake of the grace of adoption, by which they are taken into the number of the children of God, and enjoy their liberties and privileges. They have His name put upon them and receive the spirit of adoption. They have access to the throne of grace with boldness and are allowed to cry, "Abba, Father." They are pitied, protected, provided for, and disciplined by Him as by a father. Yet, they are never cast off, but are sealed to the day of redemption, and inherit the promises as heirs of everlasting salvation.[64]

XIII. SANCTIFICATION

1. THOSE WHO ARE UNITED TO CHRIST, having been effectually called and regenerated, having a new heart and a new spirit created in them through the virtue of Christ's death and resurrection, are also further sanctified in a very real and personal way, through the same virtue, and by His Word and Spirit dwelling in them, the dominion of the whole body of sin is destroyed. The different lusts of the body are increasingly weakened and mortified, and Christ's people are increasingly revived and strengthened in all saving graces, to practice all true holiness, without which no man shall see the Lord.[65]

2. This sanctification extends throughout the whole man, yet it remains imperfect in this life. Some remnants of corruption still live in every part, and from this rises a continual and irreconcilable war between the flesh and the Spirit: the flesh lusting against the Spirit, and the Spirit against the flesh.[66]

3. In this war, although the remaining corruption for a time may greatly prevail, the regenerate part overcomes through the continual supply of strength from the sanctifying Spirit of Christ. Therefore, the saints grow in grace, perfecting holiness in the fear of God, and pressing after a heavenly life in evangelical obedience to all the commands which Christ as Head and King, in His Word, has prescribed to them.[67]

XIV. SAVING FAITH

1. THE GRACE OF FAITH, by which the elect are enabled to believe, so that their souls are saved, is the work of the Spirit of Christ in their hearts, and is ordinarily brought into being by the ministry of the Word. It is also increased and strengthened by the administration of baptism and the Lord's Supper, prayer, and other means appointed of God.[68]

2. By this faith a Christian believes whatever is revealed in God's Word to be true because this Word has the authority of God Himself. The Christian also apprehends an excellence in the Word higher than all other writings and everything else in the world,

because the Word expresses the glory of God in His attributes, the excellence of Christ in His nature and offices, and the power and fullness of the Holy Spirit in His workings and operations. Therefore, the Christian is enabled to cast his soul upon the Truth he has believed, and to see and respond to the different kinds of teaching that different passages of Scripture contain. Saving faith equips him to yield obediently to the commands, tremble at its threats, and embraces the promises of God for this life and the life to come. But the first and most important acts of saving faith have immediate relation to Christ, when the soul accepts, receives, and rests upon Him alone for justification, sanctification, and eternal life, by virtue of the covenant of grace.[69]

3. Although it differs in degrees and may be weak or strong, even at its weakest, this faith is in an entirely different class and has a different nature (like other aspects of saving grace) from the kind of faith and common grace possessed by temporary believers. Therefore, though it may be frequently attacked and weakened, it is victorious, growing up in many to the attainment of a full assurance through Christ, who is both the author and finisher of our faith.[70]

XV. REPENTANCE UNTO LIFE & SALVATION

1. OF THE ELECT who are converted in more seasoned years, having lived for a time in the state of nature, and in this state served diverse lusts and pleasures, God gives repentance that leads unto life, through an effectual call.[71]

2. Because there is not one person that does good and does not commit sin, and because the best of men may fall into great sins and provocations through the power and deceitfulness of their own indwelling corruption and prevalence toward temptation, God has mercifully provided in the covenant of grace that when believers sin and fall, they shall be renewed through repentance unto salvation.[72]

3. This saving repentance is an evangelical grace by which a person who is made to feel, by the conviction of the Holy Spirit, the numerous evils of his sin, and being given faith in Christ,

humbles himself over his sin with godly sorrow, utter hatred of his sin and self-disgust, praying for pardon and strength of grace, with a purpose and effort, by supplies of the Spirit's power, to walk before God and to totally please Him in all things.[73]

4. As repentance is to be continued through the whole course of our lives, because of the body of death and the motions of it, it is every man's duty to repent of his specific known sins particularly.[74]

5. Such is the provision that God made through Christ in the covenant of grace for the preservation of believers unto salvation; that although even the smallest sin deserves damnation, there is no sin so great that it shall bring damnation on them that repent. This makes the constant preaching of repentance necessary.[75]

XVI. GOOD WORKS

1. GOOD WORKS are only those works that God has commanded in His Holy Word. Works authorized or justified by Scripture and are devised by men out of blind zeal, or upon any pretence of good intentions, are not good works.[76]

2. These good works, done in obedience to God's commandments, are the fruits and evidences of a true and living faith. By these good works believers express and show their thankfulness, strengthen their assurance, edify their brethren, beautify the profession of the Gospel, stop the mouths of the adversaries, and glorify God, whose workmanship they are; created in Christ Jesus to perform good works, and to have fruits of holiness which lead to eternal life.[77]

3. Their ability to do good works does not in any way come from themselves, but comes completely from the Spirit of Christ. To enable them to do good works, alongside the graces they have already received, a further real influence is necessary by the same Holy Spirit to cause them to will and to do God's good pleasure. Yet, believers are not, on these grounds, to grow negligent, as if they were not obligated to perform any duty, unless upon a special motion of the Spirit, but they must be diligent in stirring up the grace of God that is in them.[78]

4. Those who reach the greatest height possible in their obedience to God in this life are still so far from being able to do above what is expected, and to do more than God requires that they fall short of much, which they are obligated to do in their duty to God.[79]

5. We cannot earn pardon from sin or eternal life at the hand of God by our best works because of the great imbalance between our best works and the glory to come, and because of the infinite distance that exists between God and us. Our works do not benefit God in any way, nor can they satisfy God concerning the debt we owe for our former sins. When we have done all we can, we have only done our duty, and are still unprofitable servants. In any case, in as much as our works are good, they originate from the work of His Spirit. Even then, our good works are so defiled by us, and mixed with so much weakness and imperfection, that they cannot survive the severity of God's punishment.[80]

6. Yet, quite apart from the fact that believers are accepted through Christ as individual souls, their good works are also accepted though Him. It is not as though believers are completely without fault and without blame in God's sight in this life, but because He looks upon them in His Son, and is pleased to accept and reward that which is sincere, although it is accompanied with many weaknesses and imperfections.[81]

7. Works done by unregenerate men, although they may essentially be things which God commands, and though they may be good and beneficial both to themselves and others, yet because they do not go forth from a heart purified by faith, and are not done in a righteous manner according to the Word of God, and because it is not their underlying purpose to glorify God, they are therefore sinful and cannot please God, nor can they make a man fit to receive grace from God. Yet, for unregenerate men to neglect such works is more sinful and displeasing to God.[82]

XVII. THE PERSEVERANCE OF THE SAINTS

1. Those whom God has accepted in the Beloved, and has effectually called and sanctified by His Spirit, and given the

precious faith of His elect, can neither totally nor finally fall from the state of grace, but they will certainly persevere in that state to the end and be eternally saved. This is because God's gifts and callings can never be withdrawn, and therefore He continues to produce and nourish in them faith, repentance, love, joy, hope, and all the graces of the Spirit which lead to immortality. Although many storms and floods will come and beat against the saints, these things shall never be able to sweep them off the rock and foundation that they are fastened upon by faith. Even though, through unbelief and the temptations of Satan, the sight and feeling of the light and love of God may be clouded and obscured from them for a time, God is still the same, and they are sure to be kept by the power of God until their salvation is complete, when they shall enjoy their purchased possession, for they are engraved upon the palm of His hands, and their names have been written in the Book of Life from all eternity.[83]

2. This perseverance of the saints does not depend upon them; that is, upon their own free will. It depends upon the immutability of the decree of election that flows from the free and unchangeable love of God the Father. It also depends upon the effectiveness of the worth, value, and intercession of Jesus Christ, and union that true saints have with Him. It depends upon the oath of God and upon His abiding Spirit. It depends upon the seed of God within them and upon the very nature of the covenant of grace. All these factors give rise to the certainty and infallibility of the security and perseverance of the saints.[84]

3. The saints, through the temptation of Satan and the world, and because their remaining sinful tendencies prevail over them, and through their neglect of the means that God has provided to preserve them, may fall into grievous sins. The saints may continue in this state for a time, so that they bring upon themselves God's displeasure and grieve His Holy Spirit, suffer the injury of their graces and comforts, have their hearts hardened and their conscience wounded, and also hurt and scandalize others. By this they bring temporal judgments upon themselves. Yet, they will renew their repentance and be preserved through faith in Christ Jesus to the end.[85]

XVIII. THE ASSURANCE OF GRACE & SALVATION

1. ALTHOUGH TEMPORARY BELIEVERS, and other unregenerate men, may vainly deceive themselves with false hopes and carnal presumptions that they are in God's favor and in a state of salvation, such a hope on their part will perish. Yet, those who truly believe in the Lord Jesus, and love Him in sincerity, that attempt to walk in all good conscience before Him, may certainly be assured in this life that they are in the state of grace, and may rejoice in the hope of the glory of God. Such a hope will never make them ashamed.[86]

2. This assurance is not merely an imaginary and probable persuasion based upon a fallible hope, but is an infallible assurance of faith founded on the blood and righteousness of Jesus Christ revealed in the Gospel. It is also founded upon the inward evidence of those graces of the Spirit in connection with definite and specific promises made in Scripture, and also on the testimony of the Spirit of adoption, witnessing with our spirits that we are the children of God; and who uses the experience of assurance to keep the heart both humble and holy.[87]

3. This infallible assurance is not so joined to the essence of faith that it is an automatic and unavoidable experience. A true believer may wait long and wrestle with many difficulties before he becomes a partaker of it. Yet, being enabled by the Spirit to know the things that are freely given to him by God, he may, without extraordinary revelation, reach this assurance by using the means of grace in the right way. Therefore it is the duty of every one to give the utmost diligence to make his calling and election sure, so that his heart may be enlarged in peace and joy in the Holy Spirit, in love and thankfulness to God, and in strength and cheerfulness for carrying out the duties of obedience. These duties are the natural fruits of this assurance; —for it is far from giving men a tendency toward slackness.[88]

4. True believers may have the assurance of their salvation in various ways shaken, diminished, and suspended. This may occur because of their negligence in preserving it, or by their falling into some special sin that wounds the conscience and grieves the Spirit. Or it may occur by some sudden or intense temptation, or by God's withdrawing the light of His countenance, and causing even those

who fear Him to walk in darkness and to have no light. Yet, true believers are never left without the seed of God and life of faith; that love of Christ and the brethren, that sincerity of heart, and that conscience about their spiritual duty. Their assurance may be revised out of these things in due time by the operation of the Spirit, and in the meantime, the presence of these graces preserve them from utter despair.[89]

XIX. THE LAW OF GOD

1. GOD GAVE TO ADAM A LAW of universal obedience written in his heart, and a very specific instruction about not eating the fruit of the tree of knowledge of good and evil. By this, Adam and all of his descendents were bound to personal, total, exact, and perpetual obedience, being promised life upon the fulfilling of the law, and threatened death upon the breaking it. At the same time Adam was furnished with power and ability to keep it.[90]

2. The same law that was first written in the heart of man continued to be a perfect rule of righteousness after the fall, and was delivered by God upon Mount Sinai, in ten commandments, and written on two tables, the first four containing our duty towards God, and the other six, our duty to man.[91]

3. Besides this law, commonly called the moral law, God was pleased to give the people of Israel ceremonial laws, containing several typical ordinances. These ordinances were partly about their worship, and in them Christ was prefigured along with His gracious attributes and qualities, His actions, His sufferings, and His benefits. These ordinances also gave instructions about various moral duties. All of these ceremonial laws were appointed only until the time of reformation, when Jesus Christ, the true Messiah and only Lawgiver, who was furnished with power from the Father for this purpose, cancelled them and took them away.[92]

4. God also gave to the people of Israel several judicial laws, which came to an end when they ceased to be a nation. These judicial laws are not binding to anyone now since they were part of the laws instituted to that nation. Their general justice and fairness, however, continue to be applicable in modern times.[93]

5. The moral law forever binds everyone to obedience, justified persons as well as others, not only with regard to the matter contained in it, but also out of respect for the authority of God the Creator, who gave the law. Christ, in the Gospel, does not dissolve this law in any way, but He considerably strengthens our obligation to obey it.[94]

6. Although true believers are not under the law as a covenant of works, to be justified or condemned by it, yet it is of great use to them as well as to others, because as a rule of life it informs them of the will of God and their duty and directs and binds them to walk accordingly. It also reveals and exposes the sinful pollutions of their natures, hearts, and lives, and so examining themselves by it, they may come to greater conviction of sin, greater humility, and greater hatred against their sin. They will also begin to see more clearly their need of Christ and the perfection of His obedience. It is also useful for the regenerate soul in order to restrain their corruptions, because of the way that it forbids sin. The threats of the law serve to show what their sins actually deserve, and what troubles may be expected in this life because of these sins even committed by regenerate people that have been freed from the curse and undiminished hardships of the law. The promises of the law also show believers God's approval of obedience, and what blessings they may expect when the law is kept and obeyed, though not as due to them by the law as a covenant of works. Likewise, if a man does good and refrains from evil simply because the law encourages him toward good and deters him from the other, is no evidence that he is under the law and not under grace.[95]

7. The previously mentioned uses of the law are not contrary to the grace of the Gospel, but they sweetly comply with it, as the Spirit of Christ conquers and enables the will of man to freely and cheerfully do those things which the will of God, revealed in the law, requires to be done.[96]

XX. THE GOSPEL & THE EXTENT OF GRACE

1. BECAUSE THE COVENANT OF WORKS was broken by sin and

made unprofitable for life, God was pleased to promise Christ, the Seed of the woman, as the means of calling the elect, and bringing to life within them faith and repentance. In this promise the substance of the Gospel was revealed and shown to be effectual for the conversion and salvation of sinners.[97]

2. It is only by the Word of God that the promise of Christ, and salvation by Him, is revealed. The works of creation and providence with the light of nature do not reveal Christ or His grace even in a general or obscure way. Therefore, those who are devoid of the revelation of Christ by the promise, or by the Gospel, are even much less enabled by the light of nature to arrive at a saving faith or repentance.[98]

3. The revelation of the Gospel unto sinners, made in different times and by various parts, with the addition of promises and instructions for the obedience required within it, as to the nations and persons to whom it is granted, is merely of the sovereign will and good pleasure of God; not being annexed by virtue of any promise to the due improvement of men's natural abilities, by virtue of common light received without it, which none ever did make, or can do so. Therefore in all ages, the preaching of the Gospel has been granted unto persons and nations, as to the extent or straitening of it, in great variety, according to the counsel of the will of God.[99]

4. Although the Gospel is the only outward means of revealing Christ and saving grace, and as such, is totally sufficient to accomplish this, yet more is necessary if men who are dead in trespasses are to be born again, brought to life, or regenerated. It is necessary for there to be an effectual overwhelming work of the Holy Spirit upon the whole soul to produce in them a new spiritual life. Without this, no other means will bring about their conversion unto God.[100]

XXI. CHRISTIAN LIBERTY & LIBERTY OF CONSCIENCE

1. THE LIBERTY WHICH CHRIST HAS PURCHASED for believers under the Gospel, consists in their freedom from the guilt of sin

and the condemning wrath of God, from the curse and hardships of the law, and in their deliverance from this present evil world, from the bondage to Satan, from dominion of sin, from the harm of afflictions, from the fear and sting of death, from the victory of the grave, and from everlasting damnation. This liberty is also seen in their free access to God, and their ability to yield obedience to Him, not out of slavish fear, but with a childlike love and willing mind.

All these freedoms were also experienced in substance by true believers under the Old Testament law; but for New Testament Christians, this liberty is further expanded, for they are free from the burden of a ceremonial law, to which the Jewish church was subjected. They also have greater confidence of access to the throne of grace and fuller communications of the free Spirit of God, than believers under the law normally experienced.[101]

2. God alone is Lord of the conscience, and has left it free from all doctrines and commandments of men, which are in any respect contrary to His Word, or not contained in it. As a result, to believe such doctrines, or obey such commands out of conscience, is to betray true liberty of conscience. The requiring of an implicit faith, an absolute and blind obedience, is to destroy liberty of conscience, as well as destroying reason also.[102]

3. Those that practice any sin upon pretence of Christian liberty, or cherish any sinful lust, pervert the main design of the grace of the Gospel unto their own destruction. They completely destroy the end of Christian liberty, which is that we, being rescued from the hands of all our enemies, might serve the Lord without fear, in holiness and righteousness before Him, all the days of our lives.[103]

XXII. RELIGIOUS WORSHIP & THE SABBATH DAY

1. THE LIGHT OF NATURE shows that there is a God who has lordship and sovereignty over all; that He is just, good and does good to all. Therefore, He is to be feared, loved, praised, called upon, trusted in, and served, with all the heart, all the soul, and with all the might. Yet, the acceptable way of worshipping the true

God has been established by Himself, and so worship is limited by His own revealed will. He may not be worshipped according to the imagination and devices of men or the suggestions of Satan. He may not be worshipped by way or use of any visible representations, or any other way not prescribed in the Holy Scriptures.[104]

2. True religious worship is to be given to God the Father, Son, and Holy Spirit, and to Him alone, not to angels, saints, or any other creatures. And since the fall, worship should not be given without a mediator or by any other mediation than that of Christ alone.[105]

3. Prayer, with thanksgiving, is one part of natural worship, and God requires this of all men. To be accepted, however, it must be made in the name of the Son, by the help of the Spirit, according to God's will. Prayer must be made with understanding, reverence, humility, fervency, faith, love, and perseverance; and when praying with others, in a known language.[106]

4. Prayer is to be made for lawful things, and for all kinds of living people, who are alive now or who shall live in the future. Prayers are not to be made for the dead. Prayers are not to be made for those of whom it may be known that they have sinned the sin unto death.[107]

5. The reading of the Scriptures, preaching and hearing the Word of God, the teaching and admonishing of one another in psalms, hymns, and spiritual songs, singing with grace in our hearts to the Lord; as well as the administration of baptism, and the Lord's Supper, are all parts of true religious worship of God. These are to be performed in obedience to Him, with understanding, faith, reverence, and godly fear. Also to be used in a holy and reverent manner on special occasions are times of solemn humiliation, fastings, and thanksgivings.[108]

6. Under the Gospel, neither prayer nor any other part of religious worship is attached to any particular place; nor is it made more acceptable by any place in which it is performed, or towards which it is directed. God is to be worshipped everywhere in spirit and in truth, whether in private families daily, in secret by each individual, or solemnly within public assemblies. These are not to be carelessly nor willfully neglected or forsaken, when God by His Word or providence calls us to them.[109]

7. As it is the law of nature, that in general a proportion of time, by God's appointment, be set apart for the worship of God, so by His Word, in a positive moral, and perpetual commandment, binding all men, in all ages, He has especially appointed one day in seven for a Sabbath to be kept holy unto Him, which from the beginning of the world to the resurrection of Christ was the last day of the week, and from the resurrection of Christ was changed into the first day of the week, which is called the Lord's day: and is to be continued to the end of the world as the Christian Sabbath, the observation of the last day of the week being abolished.[110]

8. The Sabbath is then kept holy unto the Lord, when men, after an appropriate preparing of their hearts, and ordering their common affairs beforehand, not only observe a holy rest all day from their own works, words and thoughts about their worldly employment and recreations, but are also taken up the whole time in the public and private exercises of His worship, and in the duties of necessity and mercy.[111]

XXIII. LAWFUL OATHS & VOWS

1. A LAWFUL OATH is an act of religious worship, in which the person declaring in truth, righteousness, and judgment, solemnly calls God to witness what he says, and to judge him according to the truth or falsity of it.[112]

2. Only by the name of God can a righteous oath be sworn, and only if it is used with the utmost fear of God and reverence. Therefore, to swear vainly or carelessly by that glorious and awesome name of God, or to swear at all by any other name or thing, is sinful, and to be regarded with disgust and intense hatred. Yet, in matters of value and importance, for the confirmation of truth, and ending all strife, an oath is warranted by the word of God. Therefore, a lawful oath being imposed by lawful authority in such circumstances can rightly be taken.[113]

3. Whosoever takes an oath warranted by the Word of God is bound to consider the seriousness of such a solemn act, and affirm or confess to nothing except that which he knows to be true. For by rash, false, and vain oaths, the Lord is provoked, and because of

them this land mourns.[114]

4. An oath is to be taken in the plain and common sense of the words, without vague speech or mental reservation.[115]

5. A vow, which is not to be made to any creature but to God alone, is to be made and performed with all the utmost care and faithfulness. But monastic vows (as in the Church of Rome) of a perpetual single life, professed poverty, and regular obedience, quite far from being degrees of higher perfection, are superstitious and sinful snares, in which no Christian is permitted to entangle himself.[116]

XXIV. THE CIVIL MAGISTRATE

1. GOD, THE SUPREME LORD AND KING OF ALL THE WORLD, has ordained civil magistrates to be under Him, over the people, for His own glory and the public good. For this purpose He has armed them with the power of the sword, for defense and encouragement of them that do good, and for the punishment of evildoers.[117]

2. It is lawful for Christians to accept and carry out the office of a magistrate when called upon. In performing such an office they are particularly responsible for maintaining peace and justice by applying the right and beneficial laws of the nation. Under the New Testament, they may lawfully engage in warfare in order to maintain peace and justice, if the war is just and essential.[118]

3. Because civil magistrates are established by God for the purposes previously mentioned, we ought to be subject to all their lawful commands as part of obedience to God, not only to avoid punishment, but also for conscience sake. We also ought to make supplications and prayers for rulers and all who are in authority, that we may live under their authority in a quiet and peaceable life, in all godliness and honesty.[119]

XXV. MARRIAGE

1. MARRIAGE is to be between one man and one woman. It is

not lawful for any man to have more than one wife, or for any woman to have more than one husband at the same time.[120]

2. Marriage was ordained for the mutual help of husband and wife, for the increase of mankind with legitimate offspring, and the preventing of uncleanness.[121]

3. It is lawful for all sorts of people to marry if they are able to give their consent with reasonable judgment. Yet, it is the duty of Christians to marry in the Lord. Therefore, those who profess true religious faith should not marry with idolaters or unbelievers. Nor should godly believers be unequally yoked by marrying those who are wicked in their life, or with those who maintain damnable heresy.[122]

4. Marriage should not to be within the degrees of blood relation or affinity forbidden in the Word of God; nor can such incestuous marriages ever be made lawful by any law of man or consent of parties, so that such persons may live together as man and wife.[123]

XXVI. THE CHURCH

1. THE CATHOLIC OR UNIVERSAL CHURCH, which may be called invisible (with respect to the internal work of the Spirit and truth of grace), consists of the entire number of the elect, all those that have been, who are, or who shall be gathered into one under Christ, who is the Head of the church. This universal church is the wife, the body, and the fullness of Him who fills all in all.[124]

2. All persons throughout the world who profess the faith of the Gospel and obedience to God by Christ on its terms, and who do not destroy their own profession by any errors that contradict or overthrow the Gospel fundamentals, or by unholy behavior, are visible saints and may be regarded as such. All individual congregations ought to be made up of such people.[125]

3. The purest churches under heaven are subject to mixture and error. Some have degenerated so much that they have ceased to be churches of Christ and have become synagogues of Satan. Nevertheless, Christ has always had, and always will have a kingdom in this world, to the end of time, consisting of those that

believe in Him and profess of His name.[126]

4. The Lord Jesus Christ is the Head of the church. In Christ, by the appointment of His Father, is fixed in a supreme and sovereign manner, all power for the calling, institution, order or government of the church. The Pope of Rome cannot be head of the church in any sense, but he is that antichrist, that man of sin, and son of perdition, that exalts himself in the church against Christ, and all that is called God; whom the Lord shall destroy with the brightness of His coming.[127]

5. In the execution of this authority by which He is so entrusted, the Lord Jesus calls out of the world unto Himself, through the ministry of His word, by His Spirit, those that are given unto Him by His Father, that they may walk before Him in all the ways of obedience, which He prescribes to them in His Word. Those who are thus called, He commands to walk together in particular societies, or churches, for their mutual edification, and the due performance of that public worship, which He requires of them in the world.[128]

6. The members of these churches are saints because they have been called by Christ, and because they visibly manifest and give evidence (in and by their profession and walking) of their obedience unto that call of Christ. Such saints willingly consent to walk together, according to the appointment of Christ, giving themselves up to the Lord, and one to another, by the will of God, in professed subjection to the ordinances of the Gospel.[129]

7. To each of these churches thus gathered, according to the Lord's mind as declared in His Word, He has given all the power and authority, which is in any way required for them to carry on the order of worship and discipline, which He has instituted for them to observe. He has also given all the rules and commands for the due and right exertion and execution of that power.[130]

8. A particular church gathered and completely organized according to the mind of Christ, consists of officers and members. The officers appointed by Christ to be chosen and set apart by the church (so called and gathered) are bishops or elders, and deacons. These are to be appointed for the specific and appropriate administration of ordinances, and execution of power or duty with which the Lord has entrusted them, and to which He has called them. This pattern of church order will continue to the

end of the world.[131]

9. The way appointed by Christ for the calling of any person fitted and gifted by the Holy Spirit for the office of bishop or elder in a church, is that he is to be chosen by the common consent and vote of the church itself. Such a person is to be solemnly set apart by fasting and prayer, with the laying on of hands of the eldership of the church (if there is any previously appointed elder or elders). A deacon called of Christ is also chosen by the common consent and vote of the church, and set apart by prayer with the laying on of hands.[132]

10. Because the work of pastors is to apply themselves constantly to the service of Christ in His churches by the ministry of the Word and prayer, and by watching for their souls as they that must give an account to Him, it is the pressing obligation on the churches to whom they minister, not only to give them all due respect, but also to impart to them a share of all their good things according to their ability. This is done to the extent that a pastor of the Lord's church may have a comfortable supply so that he would not have to be entangled in secular affairs, and that he may also extend hospitality towards others. This is required by the law of nature, and by the express order of our Lord Jesus, who has ordained that they that preach the Gospel should live by the Gospel.[133]

11. Although an obligation rests upon the elders or pastors of the churches to urgently preach the Word by virtue of their office, the work of preaching the Word is not so exclusively confined to them. Others, who are also gifted and fitted by the Holy Spirit for the task, and approved and called by the church, may and ought to perform it.[134]

12. All believers are bound to join themselves to particular churches when and where they have opportunity to do so. All those admitted into the privileges of a church are also under the decisions, verdicts, judgments and government of that church in accordance with the rule of Christ.[135]

13. No church members, because they have been offended by a fellow member, once they have performed their prescribed duty towards the person who has caused the offense, may disturb any church order in any way, or be absent from the meetings of the church or administration of any ordinances on account of any such

offence. On the contrary, they are to wait upon Christ in the further proceeding of the church.[136]

14. Each church and all of its members are obligated to pray continually for the good and prosperity of all the churches of Christ everywhere, and seek every occasion to advance every person who comes within his or her district or calling by exercising their gifts and graces. It clearly follows that when churches are planted by the providence of God, they also ought to hold fellowship among themselves to promote peace, increasing love and mutual edification as, and when, they enjoy an opportunity to do so to their advantage.[137]

15. In cases of difficulties or differences which concern the churches in general, or any single church in particular, either in point of doctrine or administration, which affects their peace, union, and edification; or any member or members of any church are injured because of any disciplinary proceedings not consistent with the Word and correct order, it is according to the mind of Christ that many churches holding communion together, meet to consider and give their advice in or about that matter in dispute through their appointed representatives, and report to all the churches concerned. These assembled representatives, however, are not entrusted with any real church power or with any jurisdiction over the churches involved in the problem. They cannot exercise any verdict or judgment over any churches or persons, or impose their determination on the churches or officers.[138]

XXVII. THE COMMUNION OF SAINTS

1. ALL SAINTS THAT ARE UNITED TO JESUS CHRIST, their Head, by His Spirit, and faith, although this does not make them one person with Him, they do have fellowship in His graces, sufferings, death, resurrection, and glory. Being united to one another in love, they have communion in each other's gifts and graces, and are obligated to the orderly performance of such public and private duties that lead to their mutual good, both in the inward and outward man.[139]

2. By their profession, saints are obligated to maintain a holy fellowship and communion in the worship of God and in performing such other spiritual services that advance their mutual edification. They are also to give relief to each other in outward things according to their different needs and abilities to meet them. According to the rule of the Gospel, this communion or fellowship, although mainly exercised by the saints in their immediate circle of fellow believers, whether in families or churches, is also to be extended to all the household of faith, as God offers opportunity. This includes all those in every place who call upon the name of the Lord Jesus Christ. Nevertheless, their communion with one another as saints does not take away or infringe upon the personal ownership that each man has in his goods and possessions.[140]

XXVIII. BAPTISM & THE LORD'S SUPPER

1. BAPTISM AND THE LORD'S SUPPER are ordinances of positive and sovereign institution, appointed by the Lord Jesus, the only Lawgiver, to be continued in His church to the end of the world.[141]

2. These holy appointments are to be administered only by those who are qualified and called to administer them, according to the commission of Christ.[142]

XXIX. BAPTISM

1. BAPTISM IS AN ORDINANCE of the New Testament, ordained by Jesus Christ. Baptism is a sign, of the person to be baptized, of his fellowship with Christ in His death and resurrection; of his being engrafted into Christ; of forgiveness of sins; and of giving up himself to God, through Jesus Christ, to live and walk in newness of life.[143]

2. Those who actually profess repentance towards God, faith in our Lord Jesus Christ, and obedience to Him, are the only proper subjects for this ordinance.[144]

3. The outward element to be used in this ordinance is water, in which the person is to be baptized in the name of the Father, and of the Son, and of the Holy Spirit.[145]

4. Immersion, or dipping of the person in water, is necessary for the due administration of this ordinance.[146]

XXX. THE LORD'S SUPPER

1. THE LORD JESUS, HIMSELF, instituted the Supper of the Lord on the same night on which He was betrayed. He ordained this Supper to be observed in His churches until the end of the world, for the perpetual remembrance, and showing forth the sacrifice of Himself in His death, confirmation of the faith of believers in all the benefits of His death, for their spiritual nourishment and growth in Him, and their further engagement in and commitment to all the duties which they owe to Him; and to be a bond and pledge of their communion with Him, and with each other.[147]

2. In this ordinance Christ is not offered up to His Father, nor is there any real sacrifice made at all for remission (of sin of the living or the dead). It is only a memorial of that one offering up of Christ by Himself upon the cross once for all, the memorial being accompanied by a spiritual offering of all possible praise to God for Calvary. Therefore, the popish sacrifice of the mass, as they call it, is a most serious abomination, which slanders and shamefully injures Christ's own sacrifice, the only true propitiation for all the sins of the elect.[148]

3. In this ordinance, the Lord Jesus has appointed His ministers to pray, blessing the elements of bread and wine, so that these elements would be set apart from their common use and made appropriate for this holy ordinance. In this service, they take and break the bread, then take the cup, and give both to the communicants, as well as partaking of both elements themselves.[149]

4. The denial of the cup to the people, the practice of worshipping the elements, the lifting them up or carrying them about for adoration, or reserving them for any pretended religious

use, all contradict the nature of this ordinance, and run contrary to the institution of Christ.[150]

5. The outward elements in this ordinance that are correctly set apart and used as Christ ordained, so closely portray Him as crucified, that they are sometimes truly (but figuratively) referred to by the names of the things they represent, such as the body and blood of Christ. Nevertheless, in substance and nature, these elements still remain truly and only bread and wine, as they were before.[151]

6. That doctrine which maintains a change of the substance of bread and wine, into the substance of Christ's body and blood, commonly called transubstantiation, by consecration of a priest, or by any other way, is repugnant not to Scripture alone, but even to common sense and reason, overthrows the nature of the ordinance, and hath been, and is, the cause of manifold superstitions, yea, of gross idolatries.[152]

7. Worthy receivers, outwardly partaking of the visible elements in this ordinance, also receive them inwardly by faith, truly and in fact, but not in a carnal manner or in a corporeal substance, feeding spiritually upon Christ crucified, and all the benefits of His death. The body and blood of Christ is not corporally or carnally present, but it is spiritually present to the faith of believers in the ordinance, just as the elements themselves are present to their outward senses.[153]

8. All ignorant and ungodly persons who are unfit to enjoy communion with Christ are equally unworthy of the Lord's Table, and therefore, cannot partake of these holy mysteries or be admitted to the Supper while they remain in that condition without committing great sin against Christ. Whoever receives the elements unworthily is guilty of the body and blood of the Lord, eating and drinking judgment upon himself.[154]

XXXI. MAN'S STATE AFTER DEATH & THE RESURRECTION

1. THE BODIES OF MEN AFTER DEATH return to dust, and undergo corruption, but their souls, which neither die nor sleep,

having an immortal subsistence, immediately return to God who gave them. The souls of the righteous are then made perfect in holiness, are received into paradise where they are with Christ, and look upon the face of God in light and glory, waiting for the full redemption of their bodies. The souls of the wicked are cast into hell, where they remain in torment and utter darkness, reserved to the judgment of the great day. The Scriptures only acknowledge these two places for souls separated from their bodies.[155]

2. At the last day, those saints who are still alive shall not sleep, but be changed. And all of the dead shall be raised up with their own bodies, the same bodies they had while they were alive, and none other; although these raised bodies will have different qualities, they shall be united again to their souls forever.[156]

3. The bodies of the unjust shall be raised to dishonor, by the power of Christ. The bodies of the just shall be raised to honor by His Spirit, and made conformable to Christ's own glorious body.[157]

XXXII. THE LAST JUDGMENT

1. GOD HAS APPOINTED A DAY in which He will judge the world in righteousness, by Jesus Christ, to whom the Father has given all power and judgment. In that day, not only will the apostate angels be judged, but all persons that have lived upon the earth will also appear before the high court of Jesus Christ, to give an account of their thoughts, words, and deeds, and to receive according to what they have done while they were living in the body, whether good or evil.[158]

2. The ultimate purpose of God's appointing this day is for the manifestation of His glorious mercy in the eternal salvation of the elect; and of His justice, in the eternal damnation of the vile, unrepentant sinners, who are wicked and disobedient. The righteous shall then go into everlasting life, and receive that fullness of joy and glory with everlasting rewards in the presence of the Lord. The wicked, however, that do not acknowledge God, and have not obeyed the Gospel of Jesus Christ, shall be cast aside into everlasting torments, and punished with everlasting

destruction, from the presence of the Lord, and from the glory of His power.[159]

3. Christ desires us to be certainly persuaded that there shall be a day of judgment, both to deter all men from sin, and also to give greater comfort to the godly in their adversity. So He will have the day unknown to men in order that they may shake off all carnal security, and always be watchful, because they don't know the hour the Lord will come. Therefore, men may also be affected in such a way to always be prepared to say, "Come Lord Jesus; come quickly. Amen."[160]

---

[1] 2 Timothy 3:15-17; Isaiah 8:20; Luke 16:29, 31; Ephesians 2:20; Romans 1:19-21; 2:14-15; Psalm 19:1-3; Proverbs 22:19-21; Romans 15:4; Hebrews 1:1; 2 Peter 1:19-20

[2] 2 Timothy 3:16

[3] Luke 24:27, 44; Romans 3:2

[4] 2 Thessalonians 2:13; 2 Timothy 3:16; 2 Peter 1:19-21; 1 John 5:9

[5] John 16:13, 14; 1 Corinthians 2:10-12; 1 John 2:20, 27

[6] 2 Timothy 3:15-17; Galatians 1:8, 9; John 6:45; 1 Corinthians 2:9-12; 11:13, 14; 14:26, 40

[7] 2 Peter 3:16; Psalm 19:7; 119:130;

[8] Romans 3:2; Isaiah 8:20; Acts 15:15; John 5:39; 1 Corinthians 14:6, 9, 11, 12, 24, 28; Colossians 3:16

[9] 2 Peter 1:20, 21; Acts 15:15, 16

[10] Matthew 22:29, 31, 32; Ephesians 2:20; Acts 28:23

[11] 1 Corinthians 8:4, 8; Deuteronomy 6:4; Jeremiah 10:10; Isaiah 48:12; Exodus 3:14; John 4:24; 1 Timothy 1:17; Deuteronomy 4:15, 16; Malachi 3:6; 1 Kings 8:27; Jeremiah 23:23; Psalms 90:2; Genesis 17:1; Isaiah 6:3; Psalms 115:3; Isaiah 46:10; Proverbs 16:4; Romans 11:36; Exodus 34:6, 7; Hebrews 11:6; Nehemiah 9:32, 33; Psalm 5:5, 6; Exodus 34:7; Nahum 1:2, 3

[12] John 5:26; Psalms 148:13; Psalms 119:68; Job 22:2, 3; Romans 11:34-36; Daniel 4:25, 34, 35; Hebrews 4:13; Ezekiel 11:5; Acts 15:18; Psalms 145:17; Revelation 5:12-14

[13] 1 John 5:7; Matthew 28:19; 2 Corinthians 13:14; Exodus 3:14; John 14:11; 1 Corinthians 8:6; John 1:14, 18; John 15:26; Galatians 4:6

[14] Isaiah 46:10; Ephesians 1:11; Hebrews 6:17; Romans 9:15, 18; James 1:13; 1 John 1:5; Acts 4:27, 28; John 19:11; Numbers 23:19; Ephesians 1:3-5

[15] Acts 15:18; Romans 9:11, 13, 16, 18

[16] 1 Timothy 5:21; Matthew 25:34; Ephesians 1:5, 6; Romans 9:22, 23; Jude 4

[17] 2 Timothy 2:19; John 13:18;

[18] Ephesians 1:4, 9, 11; Romans 8:30; 2 Timothy 1:9; 1 Thessalonians 5:9; Romans 9:13, 16; Ephesians 2:5, 12

[19] 1 Peter 1:2; 2 Thessalonians 2:13; 1 Thessalonians 5:9; Romans 8:30; 2 Thessalonians 2:13; 1 Peter 1: 5; John 10:26; John 17:9; John 6:64

[20] 1 Thessalonians 1:4, 5; 2 Peter 1:10; Ephesians 1:6; Romans 11:33; Romans 11:5, 6, 20; Luke 10:20

[21] John 1:2, 3; Hebrews 1:2; Job 26:13; Romans 1:20; Colossians 1:16; Genesis 1:31

[22] Genesis 1:27; Genesis 2:7; Ecclesiastes 7:29; Genesis 1:26; Romans 2:14, 15; Genesis 3:6

[23] Genesis 2:17; Genesis 1:26, 28

[24] Hebrews 1:3; Job 38:11; Isaiah 46:10; Psalm 135:6; Matthew 10:29-31; Ephesians 1:11

[25] Acts 2:23; Proverbs 16:33; Genesis 8:22

[26] Acts 27:31, 44; Isaiah 55:10; Hosea 1:7; Romans 4:9-21; Daniel 3:27

[27] Romans 11:32-34; 2 Samuel 24:1; 1 Chronicles 21:1; 2 Kings 19:28; Psalms 76:10; Genesis 1:20; Isaiah 10:6, 7, 12; Psalms 1:21; 1 John 2:16

[28] 2 Chronicles 32:25, 26, 31; 2 Corinthians 12:7-9; Romans 8:28

[29] Romans 1:24-26, 28; Romans 11:7, 8; Deuteronomy 29:4; Matthew 13:12; Deuteronomy 2:30; 2 Kings 8:12, 13; Psalms 81:11, 12; 2 Thessalonians 2:10-12; Exodus 8:15, 32; Isaiah 6:9, 10; 1 Peter 2:7, 8

[30] 1 Timothy 4:10; Amos 9:8, 9; Isaiah 43:3-5

[31] Genesis 2:16, 17; Genesis 3:12, 13; 2 Corinthians 11:3

[32] Romans 3:23; Romans 5:12 &etc; Titus 1:15; Genesis 6:5; Jeremiah 17:9; Romans 3:10-19

[33] Romans 5:12-19; 1 Corinthians 15:21, 22, 45, 49; Psalms 51:5; Job 14:4; Ephesians 2:3; Romans 6:20; Romans 5:12; Hebrews 2:14, 15; 1 Thessalonians 1:10

[34] Romans 8:7; Colossians 1:21; James 1:14, 15; Matthew 15:19

[35] Romans 7:18, 23; Ecclesiastes 7:20; 1 John 1:8; Romans 7:23-25; Galatians 5:17

[36] Luke 17:10; Job 35:7, 8

[37] Genesis 2:17; Galatians 3:10; Romans 3:20, 21; Romans 8:3; Mark 16:15, 16; John 3:16; Ezekiel 36:26; John 6:44; Psalm 110:3

[38] Genesis 3:15; Hebrews 1:1; 2 Timothy 1:9; Titus 1:2; Hebrews 11:6, 13; Romans 4:1, 2 &etc; Acts 4:12; John 8:56

[39] Isaiah 42:1; 1 Peter 1:19, 20; Acts 3:22; Hebrews 5:5, 6; Psalm 2:6; Luke 1:33; Ephesians 1:22, 23; Hebrews 1:2; Acts 17:31; Isaiah 53:10; John 17:6; Romans 8:30

[40] John 1:14; Galatians 4:4; Romans 8:3; Hebrews 2:14, 16, 17; Hebrews 4:15; Matthew 1:22, 23; Luke 1:27, 31, 35; Romans 9:5; 1 Timothy 2:5

[41] Psalms 45:7; Acts 10:38; John 3:34; Colossians 1:9; 2:3; Hebrews 7:26; John 1:14; Hebrews 5:5; 7:22; John 5:22, 27; Matthew 28:18; Acts 2:36

[42] Psalm 40:7, 8; Hebrews 10:5-10; John 10:18; Galatians 4:4; Matthew 3:15; Galatians 3:13; Isaiah 53:6; 1 Peter 3:18; 2 Corinthians 5:21; Matthew 26:37, 38; Luke 22:44; Matthew 27:46; Acts 13:37; 1 Corinthians 15:3, 4; John 20:25, 27; Mark 16:19; Acts 1:9-11; Romans 8:34; Hebrews 9:24; Acts 10:42; Romans 14:9, 10; Acts 1:11; 2 Peter 2:4

[43] Hebrews 9:14; 10:14; Romans 3:25, 26; John 17:2; Hebrews 9:15

[44] 1 Corinthians 4:10; Hebrews 4:2; 1 Peter 1:10, 11; Revelation 13:8; Hebrews 13:8

[45] John 3:13; Acts 20:28

[46] John 6:37; 10:15, 16; 17:9; Romans 5:10; John 17:6; Ephesians 1:9; 1 John 5:20; Romans 8:9, 14; Psalm 110:1; 1 Corinthians 15:25, 26; John 3:8; Ephesians 1:8

[47] 1 Timothy 2:5

[48] John 1:18; Colossians 1:21; Galatians 5:17; Psalms 110:3; John 16:8; Luke 1:74, 75

[49] Matthew 17:12; James 1:14; Deuteronomy 30:19

[50] Ecclesiastes 7:29; Genesis 3:6

[51] John 6:44; Romans 5:6; 8:7; Ephesians 2:1, 5; Titus 3:3-5

[52] Colossians 1:13; John 8:36; Philippians 2:13; Romans 7:15, 18, 19, 21, 23

[53] Ephesians 4:13

[54] Romans 8:30; 11:7; Ephesians 1:10, 11; 2 Thessalonians 2:13, 14; Ephesians 2:1-6; Acts 26:18; Ephesians 1:17; Ezekiel 36:26; Deuteronomy 30:6; Ezekiel 36:27; Ephesians 1:19; Psalm 110:3; Song of Songs 1:4

[55] 2 Timothy 1:9; Ephesians 2:8; 1 Corinthians 2:14; Ephesians 2:5; John 5:25; Ephesians 1:19, 20

[56] John 3:3, 5, 6, 8

[57] Matthew 22:14; Matthew 13:20, 21; Hebrews 6:4, 5; John 6:44, 45, 65; 1 John 2:24, 25; Acts 4:12; John 4:22; John 17:3

[58] Romans 3:24; Romans 8:30; Romans 4:5-8; Ephesians 1:7; 1 Corinthians 1:30, 31; Romans 5:17-19; Philippians 3:8, 9; Ephesians 2:8-10; John 1:12; Romans 5:17

[59] Romans 3:28; Galatians 5:6; James 2:17, 22, 26

[60] Hebrews 10:14; 1 Peter 1:18, 19; Isaiah 53:5, 6; Romans 8:32; 2 Corinthians 5:21; Romans 3:26; Ephesians 1:6, 7; Ephesians 2:7

[61] Galatians 3:8; 1 Peter 1:2; 1 Timothy 2:6; Romans 4:25; Colossians 1:21, 22; Titus 3:4-7

[62] Matthew 6:12; 1 John 1:7, 9; John 10:28; Psalm 89:31-33; Psalm 32:5; Psalm 51: 1-19; Matthew 26:75

[63] Galatians 3:9; Romans 4:22-24

[64] Ephesians 1:5; Galatians 4:4, 5; John 1:12; Romans 8:17; 2 Corinthians 6:18; Revelation 3:12; Romans 8:15; Galatians 4:6; Ephesians 2:18; Psalm 103:13; Proverbs 14:26; 1 Peter 5:7; Hebrews 12:6; Isaiah 54:8, 9; Lamentations 3:31; Ephesians 4:30; Hebrews 1:14; Hebrews 6:12

[65] Acts 20:32; Romans 6:5, 6; John 17:17; Ephesians 3:16-19; 1 Thessalonians 5:21-23; Romans 6:14; Galatians 5:24; Colossians 1:11; 2 Corinthians 7:1; Hebrews 12:14

[66] 1 Thessalonians 5:23; Romans 7:18, 23; Galatians 5:17; 1 Peter 2:11

[67] Romans 7:23; Romans 6:14; Ephesians 4:15, 16; 2 Corinthians 3:18; 2 Corinthians 7:1

[68] 2 Corinthians 4:13; Ephesians 2:8; Romans 10:14, 17; Luke 17:5; 1 Peter 2:2; Acts 20:32

[69] Acts 24:14; Psalm 27:7-10; Psalm 119:72; 2 Timothy 1:12; John 14:14; Isaiah 66:2; Hebrews 11:13; John 1:12; Acts 16:31; Galatians 2:20; Acts 15:11

[70] Hebrews 5:13, 14; Matthew 6:30; Romans 4:19, 20; 2 Peter 1:1; Ephesians 6:16; 1 John 5:4, 5; Hebrews 6:11, 12; Colossians 2:2; Hebrews 12:2

[71] Titus 3:2-5

[72] Ecclesiastes 7:20; Luke 22:31, 32

[73] Zechariah 12:10; Acts 11:18; Ezekiel 36:31; 2 Corinthians 7:11; Psalm 119:6, 128

[74] Luke 19:8; 1 Timothy 1:13, 15

[75] Romans 6:23; Isaiah 1:16-18; Isaiah 55:7

[76] Micah 6:8; Hebrews 13:21; Matthew 15:9; Isaiah 29:13

[77] James 2:18, 22; Psalm 116:12, 13; 1 John 2:3, 5; 2 Peter 1:5-11; Matthew 5:16; 1 Timothy 6:1; 1 Peter 2:15; Philippians 1:11; Ephesians 2:10; Romans 6:22

[78] John 15:4, 5; 2 Corinthians 3:5; Philippians 2:13; Philippians 2:12; Hebrews 6:11, 12; Isaiah 64:7

[79] Job 9:2, 3; Galatians 5:17; Luke 17:10

[80] Romans 3:20; Ephesians 2:8, 9; Romans 4:6; Galatians 5:22, 23; Isaiah 64:6; Psalms 143:2

[81] Ephesians 1:6; 1 Peter 2:5; Matthew 25:21, 23; Hebrews 6:10

[82] 2 Kings 10:31; 1 Kings 21:27, 29; Genesis 4:5; Hebrews 11:4, 6; 1 Corinthians 13:1; Matthew 6:2, 5; Amos 5:21, 22; Romans 9:16; Titus 3:5; Job 21:14, 15; Matthew 25:41-43

[83] John 10:28; Philippians 1:6; 2 Timothy 2:19; 1 John 2:19; Psalm 89:31, 32; 1 Corinthians 11:32; Malachi 3:6

[84] Romans 8:30; Romans 9:11, 16; Romans 5:9, 10; John 14:19; Hebrews 6:17, 18; 1 John 3:9; Jeremiah 32:40

[85] Matthew 26:70, 72, 74; Isaiah 64:5, 9; Ephesians 4:30; Psalm 51:10; Psalm 32:3, 4; 2 Samuel 12:14; Luke 22:32, 61, 62

[86] Job 8:13, 14; Matthew 7:22, 23; 1 John 2:3; 1 John 3:14, 18, 19, 21, 24; 1 John 5:13; Romans 5:2, 5

[87] Hebrews 6:11, 19; Hebrews 6:17, 18; 2 Peter 1:4, 5, 10, 11; Romans 8:15, 16; 1 John 3:1-3

[88] Isaiah 50:10; Psalm 88:1-18; Psalm 77:1-12; 1 John 4:13; Hebrews 6:11, 12; Romans 5:1, 2, 5; Romans 14:17; Psalm 119:32; Romans 6:1, 2; Titus 2:11, 12, 14

[89] Song of Songs 5:2, 3, 6; Psalm 51:8, 12, 14; Psalm 116:11; Psalm 77:7, 8; Psalm 31:22; Psalm 30:7; 1 John 3:9; Luke 22:32; Psalm 42:5, 11; Lamentation 3:26-31

[90] Genesis 1:27; Ecclesiastes 7:29; Romans 10:5; Galatians 3:10, 12

[91] Romans 2:14, 15; Deuteronomy 10:4

[92] Hebrews 10:1; Colossians 2:17; 1 Corinthians 5:7; Colossians 2:14, 16, 17; Ephesians 2:14, 16

[93] 1 Corinthians 9:8-10

[94] Matthew 5:17-19; Romans 3:31; 13:8-10; James 2:8, 10-12

[95] Romans 6:12-14; Galatians 2:16; Romans 8:1; Romans 10:4; Romans 3:20; Romans 7:7, &etc.; 1 Peter 3:8-13

[96] Galatians 3:21; Ezekiel 36:37

[97] Genesis 3:15; Revelation 13:8

[98] Romans 1:17; Romans 10:14, 15, 17; Proverbs 29:18; Isaiah 25:7; Isaiah 60:2, 3

[99] Psalm 147:20; Acts 16:7; Romans 1:18-32

[100] Psalm 110:3; 1 Corinthians 2:14; Ephesians 1:19, 20; John 6:44; 2 Corinthians 4:4, 6

[101] Galatians 3:13; Galatians 1:4; Acts 26:18; Romans 8:3; Romans 8:28; 1 Corinthians 15:54-57; 2 Thessalonians 1:10; Romans 8:15; Luke 1:73-75; 1 John 4:8; Galatians 3:9, 14; John 7:38, 39; Hebrews 10:19-21

[102] James 4:12; Romans 14:4; Acts 4:19, 29; 1 Corinthians 7:23; Matthew 15:9; Colossians 2:20, 22, 23; 1 Corinthians 3:5; 2 Corinthians 1:24

[103] Romans 6:1, 2; Galatians 5:13; 2 Peter 2:18, 21

[104] Jeremiah 10:7; Mark 12:33; Deuteronomy 12:32; Exodus 20:4-6

[105] Matthew 4:9, 10; John 6:23; Matthew 28:19; Romans 1:25; Colossians 2:18; Revelation 19:10; John 14:6; 1 Timothy 2:5

[106] Psalm 95:1-7; Psalm 65:2; John 14:13, 14; 1 John 5:14; Romans 8:26; 1 Corinthians 14:16, 17

[107] 1 Timothy 2:1, 2; 2 Samuel 7:29; 2 Samuel 12:21-23; 1 John 5:16

[108] 1 Timothy 4:13; 2 Timothy 4:2; Luke 8:18; Colossians 3:16; Ephesians 5:19; Matthew 28:19, 20; 1 Corinthians 11:26; Esther 4:16; Joel 2:12; Exodus 15:1-19; Psalm 107:1-43

[109] John 4:21; Malachi 1:11; 1 Timothy 2:8; Acts 10:2; Matthew 6:11; Psalm 55:17; Matthew 6:6; Hebrews 10:25; Acts 2:42

[110] Exodus 20:8; 1 Corinthians 16:1, 2; Acts 20:7; Revelation 1:10

[111] Isaiah 58:13; Nehemiah 13:15-22; Matthew 12:1-13

[112] Exodus 20:7; Deuteronomy 10:20; Jeremiah 4:2; 2 Chronicles 6:22, 33

[113] Matthew 5:34, 37; James 5:12; Hebrews 6:16; 2 Corinthians 1:23; Nehemiah 13:25

[114] Leviticus 19:12; Jeremiah 23:10

[115] Psalm 24:4

[116] Psalm 76:11; Genesis 28:20-22; 1 Corinthians 7:2, 9; Ephesians 4:28; Matthew 19:11

[117] Romans 13:1-4

[118] Psalm 82:3; 2 Samuel 23:3; Luke 3:14

[119] Romans 13:5-7; 1 Peter 2:17; 1 Timothy 2:1, 2

[120] Genesis 2:24; Malachi 2:15; Matthew 19:5, 6

[121] Genesis 2:18; Genesis 1:28; 1 Corinthians 7:2, 9

[122] Hebrews 13:4; 1 Timothy 4:3; 1 Corinthians 7:39; Nehemiah 13:15-27

[123] Leviticus 18:1-30; Mark 6:18; 1 Corinthians 5:1

[124] Hebrews 12:23; Colossians 1:18; Ephesians 1:10, 22, 23; Ephesians 5:23, 27, 32

[125] 1 Corinthians 1:2; Acts 11:26; Romans 1:7; Ephesians 1:20-22

[126] 1 Corinthians 5; Revelation 2; Revelation 3; Revelation 18:2; 2 Thessalonians 2:11, 12; Matthew 16:18; Psalm 72:17; Psalm 102:28; Revelation 12:17

[127] Matthew 28:18-20; Ephesians 4:11, 12; Colossians 1:18; 2 Thessalonians 2:2-9

[128] John 10:16; John 12:32; Matthew 28:20; Matthew 18:15-20

[129] Romans 1:7; 1 Corinthians 1:2; Acts 2:41, 42; Acts 5:13, 14; 2 Corinthians 9:13

[130] Matthew 18:17, 18; 1 Corinthians 5:4, 5; 1 Corinthians 5:13; 2 Corinthians 2:6-8

[131] Acts 20:17, 28; Philippians 1:1

[132] Acts 14:23; 1 Timothy 4:14; Acts 6:3, 5, 6

[133] Acts 6:4; Hebrews 13:17; 1 Timothy 5:17, 18; Galatians 6:6, 7; 2 Timothy 2:4; 1 Timothy 3:2; 1 Corinthians 9:6-14

[134] Acts 11:19-21; 1 Peter 4:10, 11

[135] 1 Thessalonians 5:14; 2 Thessalonians 3:6, 14, 15

[136] Matthew 18:15-17; Ephesians 4:2, 3

[137] Ephesians 6:18; Psalm 122:6; Romans 16:1, 2; 3 John 8-10

[138] Acts 15:2, 4, 6, 22, 23, 25; 2 Corinthians 1:24; 1 John 4:1

[139] 1 John 1:3; John 1:16; Philippians 3:10; Romans 6:5, 6; Ephesians 4:15, 16; 1 Corinthians 12:7; 1 Corinthians 3:21-23; 1 Thessalonians 5:11; Romans 1:12; 1 John 3:17, 18; Galatians 6:10

[140] Hebrews 10:24, 25; Hebrews 3:12, 13; Acts 11:29, 30; Ephesians 6:4; 1 Corinthians 12:14-27; Acts 5:4; Ephesians 4:28

[141] Matthew 28:19, 20; 1 Corinthians 11:26

[142] Matthew 28:19; 1 Corinthians 4:1

[143] Romans 6:3-5; Colossians 2:12; Galatians 3:27; Mark 1:4; Acts 22:16; Romans 6:4

[144] Mark 16:16; Acts 8:36; Acts 2:41; Acts 8:12; Acts 18:18

[145] Matthew 28:19, 20; Acts 8:38

[146] Matthew 3:16; John 3:23

[147] 1 Corinthians 11:23-26; 1 Corinthians 10:16, 17, 21

[148] Hebrews 9:25, 26, 28; 1 Corinthians 11:24; Matthew 26:26, 27

[149] 1 Corinthians 11:23-26

[150] Matthew 26:26-28; Matthew 15:9; Exodus 20:4, 5

[151] 1 Corinthians 11:27; 1 Corinthians 11:26-28

[152] Acts 3:21; Luke 14:6; 1 Corinthians 11:24, 25

[153] 1 Corinthians 10:16; 1 Corinthians 11:23-26

[154] 2 Corinthians 6:14, 15; 1 Corinthians 11:29; Matthew 7:6

[155] Genesis 3:19; Ecclesiastes 12:7; Luke 16:23, 24; 23:43; Acts 13:36; 2 Corinthians 5:1, 6, 8; Philippians 1:23; Hebrews 12:23; 1 Peter 3:19; Jude 6, 7

[156] 1 Corinthians 15:51, 52; 1 Thessalonians 4:17; Job 19:26, 27; 1 Corinthians 15:42, 43

[157] Acts 24:15; John 5:28, 29; Philippians 3:21

[158] Acts 17:31; John 5:22, 27; 1 Corinthians 6:3; Jude 6; 2 Corinthians 5:10; Ecclesiastes 12:14; Matthew 12:36; Romans 14:10, 12; Matthew 25:32-46

[159] Romans 9:22, 23; Matthew 25:21, 34; 2 Timothy 4:8; Matthew 25:46; Mark 9:48; 2 Thessalonians 1:7-10

[160] 2 Corinthians 5:10, 11; 2 Thessalonians 1:5-7; Mark 13:35-37; Luke 12:35-40; Revelation 22:20

7.

SELECTED HYMNS & PSALMS

The hymns selected for this devotional booklet are classic, well-known hymns with great theological truth. Among the hymn writers included in this volume are Martin Luther, John Bunyan, John Newton, William Cowper, and Augustus Toplady.

The Scottish Psalter was written anonymously in 1635 and published and appointed for use in worship by the Church of Scotland in 1650. Scripture paraphrases were added in 1781. The Scottish Psalter and Paraphrases was the primary hymnal used by the Church of Scotland through the 19th century. The Scottish Psalter was originally contained in one volume. When the Scripture paraphrases were added in the 18th century, its addition expanded the singular volume.

SELECTIONS

"Faith's Review and Expectation"

also known as "Amazing Grace"

by John Newton (1725-1807)

C.M. 8.6.8.6. (New Britain)

Amazing grace! How sweet the sound,
That saved a wretch like me!
I once was lost but now am found
Was blind, but now I see.

'Twas grace that taught my heart to fear,
And grace my fears relieved;
How precious did that grace appear
The hour I first believed!

Through many dangers, toils, and snares,
I have already come;
'Tis grace hath brought me safe thus far,
And grace will lead me home.

The Lord has promised good to me,
His word my hope secures;
He will my shield and portion be
As long as life endures.

Yes, when this flesh and heart shall fail,
And mortal life shall cease,
I shall possess, within the veil,
A life of joy and peace.

The earth shall soon dissolve like snow,
The sun forbear to shine;
But God, who called me here below,
Will be forever mine.

"A Living and Dying Prayer for the Holiest Believer in the World"
also known as "Rock of Ages"

by Augustus Toplady (1740-1778)

7.7.7.7.7.7. (Toplady)

Rock of Ages, cleft for me,
Let me hide myself in Thee;
Let the water and the blood,
From Thy riven side which flowed,
Be of sin the double cure,
Save from wrath and make me pure.

Not the labours of my hands
Can fulfill Thy law's demands;
Could my zeal no respite know,
Could my tears forever flow,
All for sin could not atone:
Thou must save, and Thou alone.

Nothing in my hand I bring,
Simply to Thy cross I cling;
Naked, come to Thee for dress;
Helpless, look to Thee for grace;
Foul, I to the fountain fly;
Wash me, Saviour, or I die.

While I draw this fleeting breath,
When my eye-strings break in death,
When I soar to worlds unknown,
See Thee on Thy judgment throne;
Rock of Ages, cleft for me,
Let me hide myself in Thee.

Then above the world and sin,
Thro' the veil, drawn right within,
I shall see Him face to face,
Sing the story, saved by grace,
Rock of Ages, cleft for me,
Let me ever be with Thee.

"Praise for the Fountain Opened"

also known as "There Is a Fountain"

by William Cowper (1731-1800)

C.M.D. 8.6.8.6.D. (Cleansing Fountain)

There is a fountain filled with blood drawn from Emmanuel's veins;
And sinners plunged beneath that flood lose all their guilty stains.
Lose all their guilty stains, lose all their guilty stains;
And sinners plunged beneath that flood lose all their guilty stains.

The dying thief rejoiced to see that fountain in his day;
And there have I, though vile as he, washed all my sins away.
Washed all my sins away, washed all my sins away;
And there have I, though vile as he, washed all my sins away.

Dear dying Lamb, Thy precious blood shall never lose its power
Till all the ransomed church of God be saved, to sin no more.
Be saved, to sin no more, be saved, to sin no more;
Till all the ransomed church of God be saved, to sin no more.

E'er since, by faith, I saw the stream Thy flowing wounds supply,
Redeeming love has been my theme, and shall be till I die.
And shall be till I die, and shall be till I die;
Redeeming love has been my theme, and shall be till I die.

Then in a nobler, sweeter song, I'll sing Thy power to save,
When this poor lisping, stammering tongue lies silent in the grave.
Lies silent in the grave, lies silent in the grave;
When this poor lisping, stammering tongue lies silent in the grave.

Lord, I believe Thou hast prepared, unworthy though I be,
For me a blood bought free reward, a golden harp for me!
'Tis strung and tuned for endless years, and formed by power divine,
To sound in God the Father's ears no other name but Thine.

"Exceedingly Great and Precious Promises"

also known as "How Firm a Foundation"

from John Rippon's *Selection of Hymns* (1787)

11.11.11.11. (Foundation)

How firm a foundation, ye saints of the Lord,
Is laid for your faith in His excellent Word!
What more can He say than to you He hath said,
You, who unto Jesus for refuge have fled?

In every condition, in sickness, in health;
In poverty's vale, or abounding in wealth;
At home and abroad, on the land, on the sea,
As thy days may demand, shall thy strength ever be.

Fear not, I am with thee, O be not dismayed,
For I am thy God and will still give thee aid;
I'll strengthen and help thee, and cause thee to stand
Upheld by My righteous, omnipotent hand.

When through the deep waters I call thee to go,
The rivers of woe shall not thee overflow;
For I will be with thee, thy troubles to bless,
And sanctify to thee thy deepest distress.

When through fiery trials thy pathways shall lie,
My grace, all sufficient, shall be thy supply;
The flame shall not hurt thee; I only design
Thy dross to consume, and thy gold to refine.

Even down to old age all My people shall prove
My sovereign, eternal, unchangeable love;
And when hoary hairs shall their temples adorn,
Like lambs they shall still in My bosom be borne.

The soul that on Jesus has leaned for repose,
I will not, I will not desert to its foes;
That soul, though all hell should endeavor to shake,
I'll never, no never, no never forsake.

“Bí Thusa ‘mo Shúile”

traditional Irish hymn also known as “Be Thou My Vision”

translated by Mary Byrne (1880-1931)

10.10.10.10. (Slane)

Be Thou my Vision, O Lord of my heart;
Naught be all else to me, save that Thou art.
Thou my best Thought, by day or by night,
Waking or sleeping, Thy presence my light.

Be Thou my Wisdom, and Thou my true Word;
I ever with Thee and Thou with me, Lord;
Thou my great Father, I Thy true son;
Thou in me dwelling, and I with Thee one.

Be Thou my battle Shield, Sword for the fight;
Be Thou my Dignity, Thou my Delight;
Thou my soul’s Shelter, Thou my high Tower:
Raise Thou me heavenward, O Power of my power.

Riches I heed not, nor man’s empty praise,
Thou mine Inheritance, now and always:
Thou and Thou only, first in my heart,
High King of Heaven, my Treasure Thou art.

High King of Heaven, my victory won,
May I reach Heaven’s joys, O bright Heaven’s Sun!
Heart of my own heart, whatever befall,
Still be my Vision, O Ruler of all.

"Who Would True Valour See"

from John Bunyan's book *The Pilgrim's Progress*

by John Bunyan (1628-1688)

6.5.6.5.6.6.6.5. (Monk)

Who would true valour see,
Let him come hither;
One here will constant be,
Come wind, come weather
There's no discouragement
Shall make him once relent
His first avowed intent
To be a pilgrim.

Whoso beset him round
With dismal stories
Do but themselves confound;
His strength the more is.
No lion can him fright,
He'll with a giant fight,
He will have a right
To be a pilgrim.

Hobgoblin nor foul fiend
Can daunt his spirit,
He knows he at the end
Shall life inherit.
Then fancies fly away,
He'll fear not what men say,
He'll labor night and day
To be a pilgrim.

"Ein Feste Burg Ist Unser Gott"

also known as "A Mighty Fortress Is Our God"

by Martin Luther (1483-1546)
translated by Fredrick Hedge (1805-1890)

8.7.8.7.6.6.6.6.7. (Ein Feste Burg)

A mighty fortress is our God, A bulwark never failing;
Our helper He, amid the flood, Of mortal ills prevailing.
For still our ancient foe
Doth seek to work us woe;
His craft and pow'r are great,
And, armed with cruel hate,
On earth is not his equal.

Did we in our own strength confide, Our striving would be losing;
Were not the right Man on our side, The Man of God's own choosing.
Dost ask who that may be?
Christ Jesus, it is He;
Lord Sabaoth, His name,
From age to age the same,
And He must win the battle.

And tho' this world, with devils filled, Should threaten to undo us,
We will not fear, for God hath willed His truth to triumph thro' us.
The Prince of Darkness grim—
We tremble not for him;
His rage we can endure,
For lo, his doom is sure,
One little word shall fell him.

That word above all earthly pow'rs, No thanks to them, abideth;
The Spirit and the gifts are ours Thro' Him who with us sideth.
Let goods and kindred go,
This mortal life also;
The body they may kill:
God's truth abideth still,
His kingdom is forever.

PSALM 1

C.M. 8.6.8.6.

1 That man hath perfect blessedness,
who walketh not astray
In counsel of ungodly men,
nor stands in sinners' way,

Nor sitteth in the scorner's chair:
2 But placeth his delight
Upon God's law, and meditates
on his law day and night.

3 He shall be like a tree that grows
near planted by a river,
Which in his season yields his fruit,
and his leaf fadeth never:

And all he doth shall prosper well.
4 The wicked are not so;
But like they are unto the chaff,
which wind drives to and fro.

5 In judgment therefore shall not stand
such as ungodly are;
Nor in th' assembly of the just
shall wicked men appear.

6 For why? the way of godly men
unto the Lord is known:
Whereas the way of wicked men
shall quite be overthrown.

PSALM 6

To the chief Musician on Neginoth upon Sheminith, A Psalm of David.

L.M. 8.8.8.8.

1 Lord, in thy wrath rebuke me not;
Nor in thy hot rage chasten me.
2 Lord, pity me, for I am weak:
Heal me, for my bones vexed be.

3 My soul is also vexed sore;
But, Lord, how long stay wilt thou make?
4 Return, O Lord, my soul set free;
O save me, for thy mercies' sake.

5 Because those that deceased are
Of thee shall no remembrance have;
And who is he that will to thee
Give praises lying in the grave?

6 I with my groaning weary am,
I also all the night my bed
Have caused for to swim; and I
With tears my couch have watered.

7 Mine eye, consum'd with grief, grows old,
Because of all mine enemies.
8 Hence from me, wicked workers all;
For God hath heard my weeping cries.

9 God hath my supplication heard,
My pray'r received graciously
10 Sham'd and sore vex'd be all my foes,
Sham'd and back turned suddenly.

PSALM 23

A Psalm of David.

C.M. 8.6.8.6.

1 The Lord's my shepherd, I'll not want.
2 He makes me down to lie
In pastures green: he leadeth me
the quiet waters by.

3 My soul he doth restore again;
and me to walk doth make
Within the paths of righteousness,
ev'n for his own name's sake.

4 Yea, though I walk in death's dark vale,
yet will I fear none ill:
For thou art with me; and thy rod
and staff me comfort still.

5 My table thou hast furnished
in presence of my foes;
My head thou dost with oil anoint,
and my cup overflows.

6 Goodness and mercy all my life
shall surely follow me:
And in God's house for evermore
my dwelling-place shall be.

PSALM 70

C.M. 8.6.8.6.

1 Make haste, O God, me to preserve;
with speed, Lord, succour me.
2 Let them that for my soul do seek
sham'd and confounded be:

Let them be turned back, and sham'd,
that in my hurt delight.
3 Turn'd back be they, Ha, ha! that say,
their shaming to requite.

4 O Lord, in thee let all be glad,
and joy that seek for thee:
Let them who thy salvation love
say still, God praised be.

5 But I both poor and needy am;
come, Lord, and make no stay:
My help thou and deliv'rer art;
O Lord, make no delay.

PSALM 100
A Psalm of Praises.

L.M. 8.8.8.8.

1 All people that on earth do dwell,
Sing to the Lord with cheerful voice.
2 Him serve with mirth, his praise forth tell,
Come ye before him and rejoice.

3 Know that the Lord is God indeed;
Without our aid he did us make:
We are his flock, he doth us feed,
And for his sheep he doth us take.

4 O enter then his gates with praise,
Approach with joy his courts unto:
Praise, laud, and bless his name always,
For it is seemly so to do.

5 For why? the Lord our God is good,
His mercy is for ever sure;
His truth at all times firmly stood,
And shall from age to age endure.

PSALM 128

A Song of Degrees.

C.M. 8.6.8.6.

1 Bless'd is each one that fears the Lord,
and walketh in his ways;
2 For of thy labour thou shalt eat,
and happy be always.

3 Thy wife shall as a fruitful vine
by thy house' sides be found:
Thy children like to olive-plants
about thy table round.

4 Behold, the man that fears the Lord,
thus blessed shall he be.
5 The Lord shall out of Sion give
his blessing unto thee:

Thou shalt Jerus'lem's good behold
whilst thou on earth dost dwell.
6 Thou shalt thy children's children see,
and peace on Israel.

PSALM 149:1-5, 9

C.M. 8.6.8.6.

1 Praise ye the Lord: unto him sing
a new song, and his praise
In the assembly of his saints
in sweet psalms do ye raise.

2 Let Isr'el in his Maker joy,
and to him praises sing:
Let all that Sion's children are
be joyful in their King.

3 O let them unto his great name
give praises in the dance;
Let them with timbrel and with harp
in songs his praise advance.

4 For God doth pleasure take in those
that his own people be;
And he with his salvation
the meek will beautify.

5 And in his glory excellent
let all his saints rejoice:
Let them to him upon their beds
aloud lift up their voice.

9 On them the judgment to perform
found written in his word:
This honour is to all his saints.
O do ye praise the Lord.

8.

DEVOTIONAL SUGGESTIONS

FIRST, THE READING of Robert Murray McCheyne's instruction for use of the "Daily Bread" Scripture readings would be worth reading aloud to the family every now and then. It will remind your family of the dangers and advantages, not only of the scripture readings, but also of the pitfalls and benefits of family devotions in general.

Please keep in mind that the Word of God is that which is of utmost importance in the family devotions. Encourage the private reading of scripture within the family without being overbearing and legalistic. Express to each member of the family the particular joys in the discoveries and illuminations the Holy Spirit brings to God's Word.

Remember that the use of the catechism and the confession of faith are merely tools; moreover, they are tools primarily for the parents rather than the children. Certainly, the reading of a creed and the recitation of the catechism will benefit your children with the Biblical doctrines that the creed and catechism have systematized, categorized, and described; nevertheless, these tools are for *parents* so that the creed and catechism may be frontlets for *your* eyes; so that the Word of God is ever before *your* face, being first upon *your* mind and foremost upon *your* heart; and thus, sweetness to *your* soul. Then, shall your spouse see the love of God in her husband's life. Then, shall your children see the love of God in their father's life.

The confession of faith need not be the only thing read in the evening. A good book by a reputable and respected author may either substitute or supplement your evening devotions. One very small book that I highly recommend is the treatise written by John Bunyan titled *Christian Behavior. The Pilgrim's Progress* by Mr. Bunyan is also an excellent family devotional supplement.

Reading short biographies of ministers and missionaries will also encourage the family during devotional times.

Seize every opportunity that you are together to be times of devotional worship before the Lord. When you sit at the table for any meal, encourage the memorization of scripture; comment upon that day's scripture reading; ask questions concerning recent scripture readings; encourage your family to ask questions about the portions read.

After having recited your catechism, read your scripture portions, confession of faith, and/or other books, biographies or articles, it would be good to close your family worship with a good classic hymn or a psalm from the Scottish Psalter.

> *See then that you walk circumspectly, not as fools but as wise, redeeming the time, because the days are evil.*
>
> —Ephesians 5:15, 16

About the Editor

Jon Cardwell lives in Anniston, Alabama with his wife, Lisa, and his daughter, Rachel. He is the pastor at Sovereign Grace Baptist Church in Anniston after having ministered as a missionary and as a missionary-pastor in the Philippines, California, and remote bush Alaska.

www.justificationbygrace.com

www.sovereigngraceanniston.com

www.vayahiypress.com

www.gospeltruthofchristcrucified.com

www.sermonaudio.com/vayahiy

For seminars, workshops or speaking engagements on family devotions, catechizing and worship, you can contact Jon J. Cardwell through:

SOVEREIGN GRACE BAPTIST CHURCH
5440 AL Hwy 202 ~ Anniston, AL 36201
Phone: (256) 275-8996
Email: jon@justificationbygrace.com

A Puritan Family Devotional

is also available containing the
1689 London Baptist Confession
in ASV, ESV, KJV, & NASB

and is also available containing the
Westminster Confession of Faith

Other Titles by Jon Cardwell

Christ and Him Crucified

Essential Spurgeon

Fullness of the Time

Lord, Teach Us to Pray

Titles Available from Vayahiy Press

The Scottish Psalter

Christian Behavior by John Bunyan

Christ as Advocate by John Bunyan

Dying Sayings by John Bunyan

Manufactured by Amazon.ca
Bolton, ON